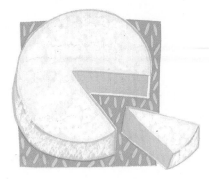

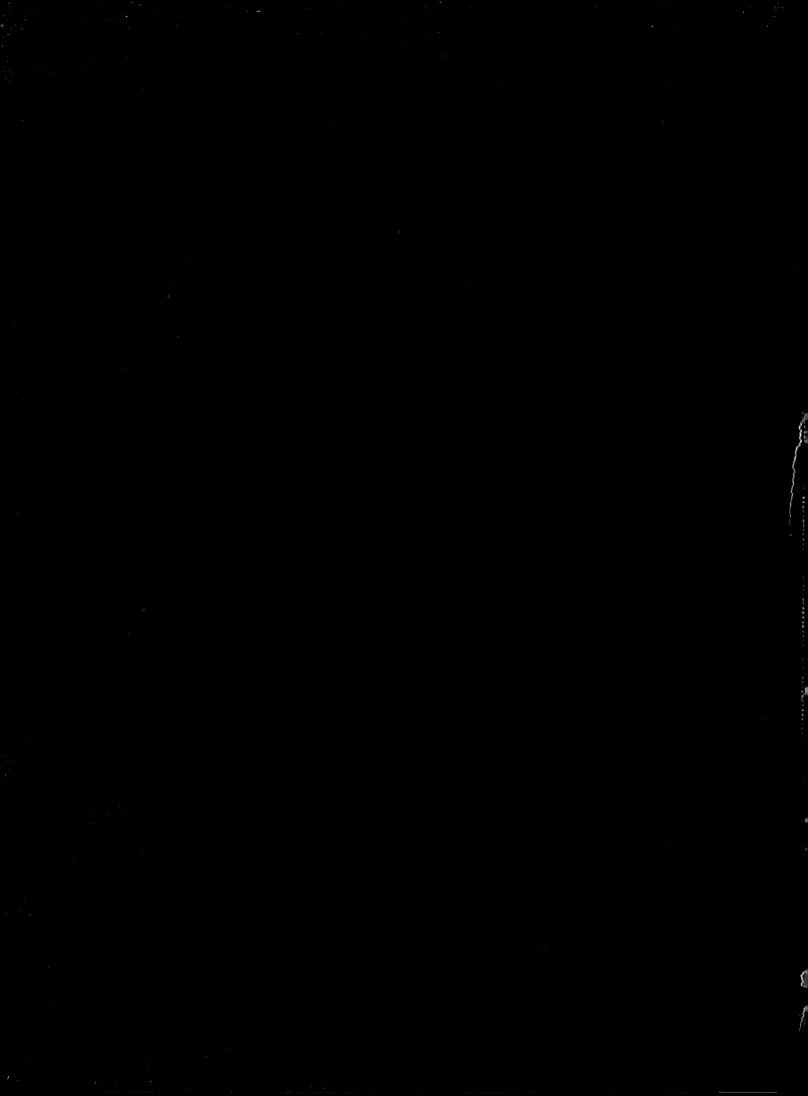

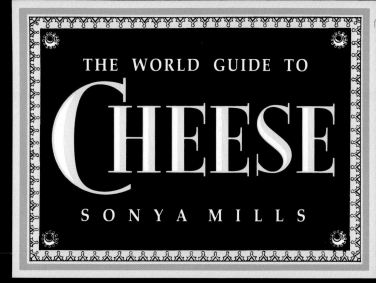

THE WORLD GUIDE TO

CHEESE

SONYA MILLS

THE WORLD GUIDE TO
CHEESE
SONYA MILLS

GALLERY BOOKS
An imprint of W.H. Smith Publishers Inc.
112 Madison Avenue
New York, New York 10016

A QUINTET BOOK
produced for
GALLERY BOOKS
An imprint of W.H. Smith Publishers Inc.
112 Madison Avenue
New York, New York 10016

ISBN 0-8317-9540-9

This book was designed and produced by
Quintet Publishing Limited
6 Blundell Street
London N7 9BH

Art Director: Peter Bridgewater
Designer: Stuart Walden
Illustrator: Annie Ellis
Editors: Josephine Bacon, Elizabeth Hurtt,
Judith Simons
Photographer: Andrew Syndenham

Typeset in Great Britain by
Central Southern Typesetters, Eastbourne
Manufactured in Hong Kong by
Regent Publishing Services Limited
Printed in Hong Kong by
Leefung-Asco Printers Limited

ACKNOWLEDGEMENTS

My grateful thanks to all the organizations listed
below who helped to make this as up-to-date and
accurate as any book about such an elusive, ever-
changing subject as cheese can ever be. Especial
thanks to my editor, Josephine Bacon, whose
infinitely greater knowledge than mine of both
food and languages solved many problems.

Central Marketing Organization of German
Agricultural Industries (UK)
Cheeses from Switzerland
The Danish Dairy Board
The Dutch Dairy Board
The English Country Cheese Council
Food and Wine from France Ltd
French Dairy Farmers Ltd
Harrods Ltd
The Italian Chamber of Commerce for
Great Britain

The publishers would like to extend their special
thanks to the **London Cheese Factory** for their
assistance in providing for photography the great
majority of cheeses featured in this book.

CONTENTS

hen I first started researching this book I thought I knew a fair bit about cheese. As the weeks went by I realized the extent of my ignorance. Not only were there hundreds of cheeses, with long histories, which I had never heard of, but I kept finding new ones, unrecorded in reference books but being bought by eager customers in quite ordinary shops.

The more I learnt about cheese the greater grew my respect for it. From a simple raw material – milk – people all over the world have learnt to make a nutritious food with an amazing variety of forms and flavours. Over the centuries cheesemaking became an art and then a science as modern technology stepped in. Soon I grew obsessed with the subject: I wrote about cheeses all day; ate a different one at breakfast, lunch and dinner and dreamed about them at night.

In the past, most cheeses were made purely for local consumption. Today they may be exported all over the world, and are also made in countries far away from their

original homes. There has never been a better time to discover the world of cheese. And what a vast world it is – even if you were to restrict yourself to French cheeses, you could eat a different one every single day of the year. Then you'd need a few more years to sample Italian, Swiss, Dutch and German ones!

This book is designed as an introduction to the fascinating world of cheese. One of the great joys of cheese is its versatility. It can be enjoyed as it comes or used in cooking. It can be eaten at any time of the day – in Holland, Scandinavia and much of the Middle East it appears at breakfast – and in any setting, from impromptu picnics to three-star restaurants. It can be a quick snack, part of a salad or the finale to a gourmet meal. When cooked, it can add flavour to a simple vegetable dish or an elaborate creation, such as a soufflé. I have concentrated on those which you have a good chance of actually buying, wherever you live. A number of new ones are included, as well as the great classics. Rare and unexported cheeses which you probably won't get the chance to try unless

you travel abroad are in a separate chapter. If you happen to be a vegetarian, or are trying to combine a passion for cheese with a need to reduce the waistline, the world of cheese is by no means closed to you; the penultimate chapter outlines what to look for.

I have not attempted to describe the taste of a cheese, beyond saying it is mild or strong, or comparing it with another familiar one. Flavours are indescribable – they must be experienced.

Sonya Mills

CHAPTER ONE

THE
WORLD
OF
CHEESE

THE DISCOVERY OF CHEESE

 hen humans stopped hunting and gathering their food and began domesticating animals, they found that the milk of ruminants or grazing animals was good to drink. In hot countries like Egypt, leftover milk must often have curdled. Doubtless some frugal soul put 'bad' milk into a cloth or small basket, drained off the liquid and found the solids good to eat. Nobody knows when it started, but chemical tests of pots from a 5,000-year-old tomb produced traces of cheese, and ancient cave paintings seem to show milk being processed.

The big step was to turn milk into cheese at will, not wait for it to happen. This needs an enzyme like rennet, secreted in the stomachs of young ruminants. Arab herdsmen probably discovered this by accident too, when milk kept in skins made from partly-cured sheep's stomachs curdled quickly and made a sweet-tasting cheese.

Gradually cheese-making arose wherever the land would support grazing animals – mainly goats, sheep and cows – to be milked. Exceptions were China, where milk was never thought to be edible, and the Indian continent, where to Hindus and Buddhists cows were sacred. Cheese was common in the Greek and Roman empires: Homer's *Odyssey* describes cheesemaking, and the Romans who occupied Britain enjoyed the local Cheshire.

By the beginning of Christian times cheesemakers had discovered how to press, ripen and cure the basic fresh white cheese to produce many different types, and the founding of medieval monasteries led to the development of new varieties of cheese, some of which, like PORT-SALUT, are still called 'monastery cheeses'.

As trade developed, cheese became an important commodity, and great cheese fairs were held throughout medieval Europe. Most cheese was still fairly perishable – soft cheeses in particular did not travel well – but the Dutch developed hard-pressed cheeses with solid rinds and were major exporters by the 14th century.

MODERN TIMES

The industrialization of cheese manufacture has not been a total gain: mass-produced cheeses are blander and less individual than farm cheeses. Though most cheese sold and eaten today is factory-made from pasteurized milk, the demand for farmhouse cheese, especially those made with unpasteurized milk, continues. (Although 'farmhouse-made' is no guarantee that unpasteurized milk has been used.) In recent years many small dairies have switched to using pasteurized milk: although modern dairy hygiene standards ensure there is next-to-no health risk, pasteurized milk is easier to handle. Further-more, in North America most states (with the exception of California and New York) prohibit the manufacture and import of raw-milk cheeses.

The history of cheese is still unfolding. Cheeses once made in only one country are now copied in many places; if names become legally protected, new names are invented for the 'foreign' copies. Every year different cheeses are invented; many are merely variations on old themes, and others are versions of existing cheeses with additions like fruits, herbs, nuts, etc. A few are genuinely different: the various blue Brie-type cheeses are an example. Some of these are mentioned in this book; whether they will survive to become tomorrow's CHEDDARS or CAMEMBERTS only time will tell.

CHEESE IN THE UNITED STATES

In North America goats, sheep and cows were unknown before the European settlers imported animals from the Old World. There were buffalo in the west but the Plains Indians were hunters, with no thought of milk or MOZZARELLA. The first settlers made copies of their national cheeses, but later developed many distinctive new ones. Since the first settlements were on the East Coast the biggest cheese-producing state then was New York, but today the title goes to

Wisconsin, which grows fodder and raises cattle to provide milk for 80% of American cheese.

In the 19th century the new pasteurizing process gave cheesemakers a raw material which was more stable and easier to control. New cheesemaking processes used pure starter cultures and standardized rennet, both eventually laboratory-made. This control over the complex bacterial and chemical processes of cheesemaking turned it into a science instead of an art, and made it a year-round affair, instead of a seasonal activity, confined to late spring and early summer. Mass production of cheese began and the United States led the way with the first cheese factories, or creameries, being set up in New York State in the 1880s.

Today the United States is the world's greatest cheese producer, though not the biggest exporter. That title goes to the Dutch, who never lost their early lead. France produces the greatest variety of cheeses; one could eat a different type of cheese every day of the year and then some – for France has over 370 varieties in commercial production!

CHEESEMAKING

Cheese production methods range from the primitive to ultra-modern. Greek shepherds still make their feta using methods scarcely changed since before Christ. In modern creameries, milk becomes cheese on semi-automatic production lines – passing from huge tanks to milling machines to presses via pipes, hoppers and conveyor belts.

Cheesemaking requires enormous amounts of milk. A medium-sized EMMENTAL, weighing about 180 lbs (80 kg), needs more than 1,760 pt (1,000 l) of milk – the output of some 80 cows. In Great Britain even farmhouse cheeses are made from milk delivered twice a day from farms in the surrounding area, so weekly output is low.

Though cheeses vary so greatly in flavour, texture and appearance they are made basically on the same general lines.

DUTCH FARMHOUSE CHEESE-MAKING

1 This clotted mixture, formed by the introduction of rennet to heated milk, is cut to separate the curds from the whey. The whey is then drained off and the curds reheated to ripen.

2 The dried curds are pushed into cheese moulds lined with muslin which allows the cheese to be turned during pressing.

3 This traditional cheese press is still used in farmhouses for the production of cheese. Edams are pressed for 2 to 3 hours and Gouda for 6 hours.

4 The cheeses are released from the moulds and submerged in a brine bath for several days. This enhances flavour, texture and prolongs preservation.

5 The cheeses are dried on unpainted wooden shelves before being protected with a porous plastic skin and left to mature.

The milk is usually pasteurized first (gently heated to just below boiling point to kill unwanted bacteria), then soured with a bacterial culture or 'starter'. For most cheeses, rennet is then added to separate the soured milk into curds and whey. (For some cheeses, mainly the soft fresh varieties, lactic [milk] acid is used instead of rennet.) The curds are stirred or cut to release the whey and may also be gently heated (scalded), raised to an even higher temperature (cooked), stacked and turned (cheddared), or washed.

After this the curds are treated in different ways – poured straight into containers or moulds or milled (ground) first; pressed hard, lightly or not at all. The final process, ripening or maturing, contributes a great deal to the final character of the cheese, depending on duration, temperature and humidity levels. Treatment during this period adds another dimension. The cheese may be left to ripen naturally; soaked in brine; waxed or plastic-coated to discourage mould growth; brushed, washed or pierced to encourage mould penetration; smoked; or covered with herbs or leaves.

SHAPE AND WEIGHT

Though much cheese today is sold ready-cut or packaged, the shape and size of the original cheese is another part of its character. Traditionally cheeses were made in six basic shapes: drum, ball, wheel or disk, rectangular block, square and roll or log. Every cheese had its established shape – CHEDDAR was always a drum, EDAM a ball. But today many factory cheeses are block-shaped for more convenient automated handling, and easier cutting. A few soft cheeses are made in fancy shapes such as hearts and pyramids.

Cheeses also come in a vast range of weights, from single-portion cream cheeses weighing about 2 oz (60 g), to mighty 286-lb (130-kg) EMMENTALS.

CLASSIFICATION OF CHEESES

General groups of cheeses like hard or soft are obvious: extreme examples would be a rock-hard PARMESAN and a super-soft cream cheese. This is the consistency of the cheese, which depends on its moisture content. They are described as fresh (eg a cottage cheese with up to 80% moisture); soft; semi-soft; semi-hard or hard (eg PARMESAN with only 28% moisture). These categories only give a broad indication, as cheeses dry out as they age – for example CHEDDAR is semi-hard when young, although classified as a hard cheese; even young PARMESAN is semi-hard when sold fresh. Cheese may also vary in consistency depending on manufacturing differences in their country of origin. Cheeses can also be classified by a number of other criteria: production method; raw materials used; fat content and ripening treatment.

RAW MATERIALS

Most cheeses today are made from cows' milk, but in countries where the land is too poor to graze cattle, goat's and sheep's (ewe's) milk is used. Each has its own distinctive tang, which may also vary with the type of pasture the animals graze on. Italy's famous MOZZARELLA cheese was once made from water-buffalo milk; now the scarcity of water-buffalo and the cheese's international popularity means that most 'Mozzarella' seen outside Italy is made wholly or partly from cow's milk. The milk used for cheese may be full-cream, partly skimmed or wholly-skimmed, which affects both taste and fat content. Most cheeses have no added ingredient except salt, but some contain herbs, spices, wine, beer, fruit or nuts, as well as other types of additives.

FAT CONTENT

This important part of classification, indicating how nourishing the cheese is, is expressed as a percentage of the cheese's dry matter, not its total weight. This is due to the moisture in a cheese reducing with age, so the percentage of fat becomes higher. For example, BRIE and GRUYÈRE have the same overall fat content – about 45% – but of two pieces of the same weight Gruyère contains more fat because it has less moisture.

Cheeses range in fat content from below 2% to over 80% but the average is 45–50%. Packaged cheeses often show the percentage on the wrapper. In the United States, the percentage of fat is followed by the letters IDM: 'in dry matter'. Some cheeses are simply labelled low, medium or full fat.

RIPENING TREATMENTS

These mostly affect the rind. Soft-ripened cheeses may have a velvety-white rind (BRIE, CAMEMBERT), or a yellowish-red rind (LIMBURGER, SAINT-PAULIN). Many hard cheeses have a natural dry rind; others have 'artificial' rinds – the wax on a VERMONT CHEDDAR or plastic on a Dutch cheese – which are not part of the cheese itself. Fresh cheeses, and those ripened inside packaging, do not have rinds. Blue cheeses are the exception, as their treatment does not affect the rind, only the inside.

BUYING CHEESE

The best place to buy cheese depends on what you are looking for. For big selections, including exotic imported and small-batch farmhouse cheeses, specialist delicatessens are best. The counter staff should be able to advise you, and let you taste samples.

Beware of pretentious shops carrying so many cheeses that turnover is slow and much of the stock is past its best. Bad signs are hard cheeses looking dry and cracked; cheeses sweating from exposure to heat or from being encased in cling film (plastic wrap); soft cheeses leaking from their rinds or having cracked, brown rinds and shrunken appearance; above all any noticeably acrid or ammonia-like smell. Though some of the washed-rind cheeses

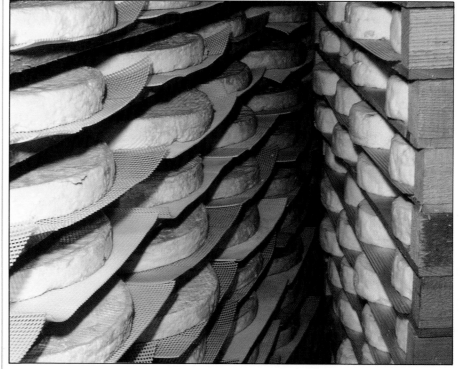

ABOVE *Brie is carefully stored to allow the cheese to mature. The ripening process produces a distinctive soft white rind.*

are distinctly smelly, and are meant to be, the overall smell of a cheese shop should be appetizing. Shop with your nose as well as your eyes!

Cheese shops are uncommon in small towns; so for many people the cheese counter of a delicatessen or grocery store, or the supermarket fresh-food and delicatessen counters, are the places to go.

The choice may not be so wide but the chances are that what is on offer should be fresh and in good condition. The problem in these situations is more likely to be under-age cheeses, too young to have developed their full flavour. (Soft-ripened cheeses like BRIE should not have 'chalky' centres.) Supermarket prices are competitive, and if you need lots of cheese for a big family or a party their fresh-cut ones are best buys.

If you are short of time and need cheese that can be stored for a while, then pre-packed cheese from the supermarket will fit the bill. To be sure of getting what you want you must be able to interpret the labelling. Vacuum-packed supermarket chunks will carry little more than name, weight and price, but the labels on boxed and wrapped cheese are full of information if you can decode them: fat content, origin, protected names, trade marks and other symbols.

Pre-packed cheeses, especially if ready-sectioned or sliced, are more expensive than those cut from a larger piece, as the packaging must be paid for. So it is useful to remember that the smaller the piece, the greater the proportion of the price goes on packaging rather than cheese.

STORING CHEESE

Ideally, cheese should not be stored at all, but bought ripe and eaten within a day or two – all very well if you are buying special cheeses for a dinner party but impractical for everyday life.

Modern homes don't offer the right conditions – a cool, even temperature and good ventilation – for storing cheese. A refrigerator is too cold and airless and outdoors is usually too warm or too cold. Common sense and compromise are the answer. In a ventilated cupboard in a cool airy kitchen, semi-hard and hard cheeses will keep perfectly well for a week if necessary. In hot weather, the refrigerator is best; factory-made cheeses will have been kept under refrigeration anyway before they reach you. Softer cheeses will be safer in the refrigerator, but only for a day or so. Put them in the warmest parts – the door or the salad drawer. Fresh cheeses should always be refrigerated.

Take refrigerated cheese out about an hour before needed or it will not have time to develop its full taste. *Never* freeze cheese. Always wrap each piece of cheese separately in cling film (plastic wrap) or foil to conserve moisture and prevent the

ABOVE *Hundreds of Gouda and Edam cheeses on sale at the famous cheese market at Alkmaar, Holland.*

flavours mingling: grease-proof or waxed paper are also useful. Very dry cheeses like PARMESAN and GRUYÈRE benefit from a wrapping of damp muslin (cheesecloth) or a dampened non-woven cloth.

Store vacuum-packed and pre-packed cheeses according to sell-by or pull dates and the manufacturer's instructions. Unopened, they will keep for a long time; once unwrapped they start to deteriorate like any other cheese.

Bits of hard cheese too old for eating need not be wasted. Wipe off any sweated-out fat and scrape away mould growth; the cheese can then be grated and used for cooking or sprinkling over food. Stale blue cheese can be mashed with butter to make a spread. The only cheeses which should be discarded are overripe soft cheeses, smelling of ammonia.

SERVING CHEESE

Cheese as a part of a meal should be served at room temperature or slightly cooler, kept wrapped until the last moment and finally attractively presented on a cheese board. A good dinner party selection should include cheeses appealing to different palates and of contrasting appearance, flavour and texture. Alternatively, you might wish to present a selection of cheeses from one country – French, Italian or domestic. A very strong-smelling cheese, like a ripe LIMBURGER, is best served on its own with a separate knife! *No* processed cheese should appear.

You need not serve an enormous number of cheeses. Four or five – say, one soft, one semi-hard, one blue, one hard and something unusual you hope guests will not have met before – provides ample choice.

Most cheeses should be cut like a cake or in tapered slices, so that the rind is evenly shared out. Brick-shaped cheeses can be cut with a cheese slice. This was originally a Scandinavian implement which looks like a cake-slice, but has a wide sharp-edged opening across the middle of the blade. Running the slice over the surface of the

brick shaves a thin piece off the top. The hard Scandinavian cheeses are always cut in this way, and it is considered very bad manners to cut hard cheese with a knife in Norway and Sweden. Never cut the tip or 'nose' off a triangle of BRIE! Whether to eat the rind or not is very much a matter of personal taste, but generally speaking those on soft ripened cheeses are good until they get very ripe. With a few exceptions those on washed-rind cheeses are inedible, unless you enjoy strong flavours. Dry, natural rinds are musty and not very nice; artificial rinds like plastic wax coatings or dried leaves are definitely inedible.

Should the cheese come before or after the dessert? Cheese first is best if wine has been served with the meal so that guests can finish it with the cheese. Otherwise do as you please. Alternatively, now that so many people are weight-watching, cheese, especially with fresh fruit, can replace dessert. Apples with CHEDDAR, pears with GORGONZOLA, grapes with Swiss cheese, soft fruit with cream cheese are all time-honoured combinations. Another possibility is a creamy dessert cheese such as MASCARPONE or NEUFCHÂTEL.

Serve the cheese with butter for those who want it and crackers (plain biscuits). Salted crackers are a mistake – cheese is salty in itself – and cheese-flavoured crackers will certainly not do justice to your selection.

For everyday, cheese is usually eaten with bread. But the bread (and cheese) you pick make all the difference. Processed cheese with white, sliced bread is strictly a filler; full-flavoured natural cheeses with wholemeal bread, French bread, and rye or granary rolls make snacks to remember.

COOKING WITH CHEESE

Meals made with a foundation of nourishing cheese are found in the cuisine of most nations. Famous dishes like quiche Lorraine, Welsh rarebit, fondue, cheese soufflé, rösti, cheesecake and, above all, pizza, have become popular far beyond their countries of origin, and recipes for them are found in countless cookbooks.

The cheese used for such dishes should ideally be the authentic one, but if this is too expensive or unavailable, another can be substituted.

Cheeses suitable for cooking are mainly the reasonably-priced everyday kinds. Anyway, it would be a waste to cook an expensive imported cheese. Thus, the following are good cheeses to cook with: all types of CHEDDAR; semi-hard regional and local cheeses; Dutch and Swiss cheeses. EMMENTAL and GRUYÈRE, Swiss cheeses, give a fine flavour and are essential for fondues. PARMESAN is ideal for sprinkling on finished dishes because it grates finely and has good flavour: added to dishes with other cheeses it helps to intensify their flavour. Processed cheeses tend to be too bland to give good results when cooked.

The secret of cooking cheese successfully is to subject it to minimal heat, so as to preserve the flavour, and to prevent it becoming tough and rubbery – in some cases it will even form long strings. When making a cheese sauce, for example, add the cheese, medium- or coarse-grated (shredded), at the very end, with just enough heat to melt it. When a high heat must be used, as when browning a cheese topping, do this as fast as possible.

BEVERAGES AND CHEESE

Wine goes naturally with cheese, but plain cheeses like CHEDDAR and strong ones like LIEDERKRANZ are better with beer or dry cider. Some people like mild cheese with a glass of milk. Spirits, such as whisky and gin, and sweet fizzy drinks don't bring out the best in cheese.

If you choose wine what type should it be? Generally a medium or dry is best. If the cheese is from Europe a wine from the same country of origin is ideal. But whether the wine is domestic or imported it should go with the character of the cheese. Really full-blooded cheeses like the blues need robust red wines; a fresh, soft cheese calls for something dry and white. That said, don't be too fussy; good cheese goes with almost any wine, except the very sweet varieties.

CHAPTER TWO

*H*ARD *C*HEESES

ard cheeses are produced by removing sufficient moisture in such a way as to achieve the desired characteristics of the cheese in question. This is done both in the way in which the curds are treated, and by curing the cheese for short or long periods – the older a cheese, the harder it is. The price of cheese is affected by these two factors: PARMESAN is costly because it takes more milk to make it than any other cheese, and because it must then be stored for at least a year before it can be sold.

Cheeses in this group are scalded – the processing is carried out at higher temperatures than those used for making soft cheeses. Those of the English type undergo a process called cheddaring. When the cheese is made by hand, the curd is removed from the vat, cut into blocks, then stacked and restacked for nearly an hour while it continues to drain, until the curd fuses into a fibrous mass. In factory production, the curd is blown into the top of a huge tower and drains under its own weight.

The curd is then put through a mill to reduce it to little pieces, and salted to add flavour and help the cheese keep well. Finally it is packed into moulds and pressed to get rid of still more whey. The mould gives the cheese its customary size and shape; most hard cheeses were traditionally made in large drums or 'wheels', but today they are more likely to be produced in blocks. The amount of pressing determines how hard the finished cheese will be.

Finally the cheese must be matured. Traditional English cheeses like CHEDDAR were knocked out of the mould and bandaged in cheesecloths or dipped in wax; today a factory-made cheese is vacuum-packed in clear plastic. Maturing takes place under carefully-controlled conditions to ensure that temperature and ventilation are just right. A traditionally-made farmhouse cheese will be turned every day for several weeks to redistribute the moisture inside; less frequently as it dries out. The length of time depends on the cheese: CAERPHILLY is ready in two weeks, while CHEDDAR may be left for 12 months or more if it is to be sold as mature.

Cheeses such as EMMENTAL are known as 'cooked' cheeses and are made to a basic recipe that differs somewhat from that of the ordinary or uncooked hard cheeses. The curd is not just scalded, but heated to a higher temperature for a longer period of time. Neither is it cheddared, but put straight into a mould, heavily pressed and floated in a brine bath for several days. Those with holes or 'eyes' in the body are ripened in warm, humid storerooms, which causes gas bubbles to form.

The very hard, grainy cheeses like PARMESAN are hard cooked cheeses matured for anything up to four years. The fat content of hard cooked cheeses ranges from 32% for the very hard Parmesan types to 50% for Beaufort.

HARD CHEESES – UNCOOKED

ASIAGO

ITALY

Because it is not cheddared, this cheese has a firm rather than hard consistency, with a scattering of holes. It is straw coloured and made in drums with a smooth pale-yellow rind stamped with the name, which is that of the place where it was originally made. The flavour is mild, and fat content lower than for most hard cheeses (34%). It is eaten as a table cheese when under 6–9 months old; after that the texture becomes granular and it is used for grating.

ASIAGO PRESSATO is a harder, pressed version.

CHEDDAR

GREAT BRITAIN

Top favourite in both the United States and Great Britain, CHEDDAR must be the most widely eaten cheese in the world. Even the French, with hundreds of far more exotic native cheeses to choose from, have their own popular version – CANTAL.

The ancestor of the CHEDDARS made today in factories in such unlikely places as Egypt and Japan was first produced in the county of Somerset and was already a highly esteemed cheese in the reign of Elizabeth I. It took its name from the nearby Cheddar Gorge. English CHEDDAR is now made in various parts of Great Britain, but genuine FARMHOUSE CHEDDARS still come from the same area.

The original CHEDDAR was made in big, sometimes huge, drums, but today is often a block. It has a natural dry rind and is golden-yellow in colour, with a firm close texture. Most is sold when it has matured

Cheddar

for 3–5 months, and is very mild. This recommends it to many people, but not to connoisseurs who dismiss it as 'mousetrap cheese'. But a mature CHEDDAR, aged for 9–12 months or longer, should be strong but mellow. FARMHOUSE CHEDDAR, especially if made from unpasteurized milk, is one of the world's greatest cheeses.

AMERICAN CHEDDAR

UNITED STATES

Over 70% of all the cheese produced in the United States is CHEDDAR, so it's not surprising that it is known loosely as 'American cheese'. The techniques of making CHEDDAR were brought over by the Pilgrim Fathers. Virtually all

AMERICAN CHEDDAR is factory-made. It comes in a wide range of shapes and sizes and may be finished with black, red or orange wax. The colour varies from almost white to a deep orange.

AMERICAN CHEDDAR is labelled mild, mature or sharp according to whether it has been aged for 2–3 months, over 4 months or 6–12 months. The average pre-packed supermarket offering is bland-to-tasteless, especially if it is processed. There are also some very good AMERICAN CHEDDARS. Some of the best known are:

CAMOSUN: A rather soft, crumbly CHEDDAR developed in Washington State around 1932.

COON: A vintage CHEDDAR, aged for 12 months or more. Dark and crumbly due to curing at a relatively high temperature.

NEW YORK CHEDDAR: Most American cheese is made from pasteurized milk as State laws prohibit the use of raw or unpasteurized milk. But this is not the case in New York State, which accordingly produces two very fine full-flavoured CHEDDARS: HERKIMER and COOPER. HERKIMER is very pale; the name, which should be stamped on the cheese, comes from the Herkimer cheese factory where it was first produced. COOPER is yellow, softer and more crumbly.

PINEAPPLE: Virtually extinct today, this CHEDDAR got its name from its shape and the criss-cross markings on its shiny rind. The effect was produced by hanging the cheese in a net while it cured, and shellacking the rind. It was first made in Litchfield County, Connecticut, in the 1840s.

TILLAMOOK: Another raw-milk CHEDDAR, this is yellow in colour and varies from mild to sharp according to age. It is made in Oregon and not widely available outside the West Coast.

VERMONT: A distinctive cheese with shiny, black-waxed rind contrasting with a pale interior. One of the best of all AMERICAN CHEDDARS.

WISCONSIN CHEDDAR: See COLBY.

COLDPACK or POTTED CHEESE is a soft version of CHEDDAR produced by grinding up and mixing together two high-quality aged cheeses. It is not heated, so is not a processed cheese. It is packed in cartons or pots and often contains added flavourings.

CANADIAN CHEDDAR

CANADA

This deserves special mention because the best of it is of extremely high quality, being made from raw milk, and is on a par with the English FARMHOUSE CHEDDARS. BLACK DIAMOND, with its black waxed rind, is world famous; some of it is aged for over 2 years. Another fine example is CHERRY HILL.

CHESHIRE

GREAT BRITAIN

One of England's oldest cheeses, dating back to Roman times, and mentioned in the Domesday Book published in the 11th century, it is more open-textured and crumbly than CHEDDAR, with a salty tang which comes from salt springs which run under the Cheshire pastures where the cattle graze. The colour can be red, white or blue. Red is simply the basic cheese coloured with annatto, and equally popular, but the blue-veined version is rare.

CHESHIRE cheese was originally made near the then village of Chester lying on the River Dee.

COLBY

UNITED STATES

A variation on the CHEDDAR theme, this is produced by a rather different process. After the whey has been drained off the curd it is washed in cold water; this increases the moisture content so that the cheese matures quickly, but also means that it does not keep well. In addition, the cheddaring process is omitted, which gives the cheese a more open, granular texture. It is named after Colby, Wisconsin, where it was first made in 1882. The flavour is mild, almost sweet, and the colour deep yellow to orange.

COLBY is also known as WASHED CURD CHEESE. Stirred curd and granular cheese are close relations.

DERBY

GREAT BRITAIN

A comparatively rare cheese today, DERBY has the distinction of being the first English

Derby

cheese to be factory-made, when the first English cheese factory opened at Longford in Derbyshire. It is pale honey-coloured, with a firm, close texture. The flavour is mild, even bland if the cheese is sold too young.

DOUBLE GLOUCESTER

GREAT BRITAIN

Named for its large size and Gloucestershire origins, this cheese was not

Double Gloucester

always the bright yellow-orange colour it usually is today. In the 18th century, cheese merchants discovered that the smart folk in London thought a rich colour indicated a rich cheese, so they painted theirs with carrot juice, beetroot juice or saffron. Nowadays it is dyed with annatto, a reddish-yellow colouring matter imported from South America. It is a full-flavoured cheese, with smooth creamy texture. There is a variety known as COTSWOLD CHEESE which has chives in it. The cheese, or something like it – made in a big wheel, with a tough rind – was known in Gloucestershire as far back as the 10th century. It was then used in spring ceremonies where cheeses were rolled down slopes. The tradition is still observed in the village of Chipping Camden.

SINGLE GLOUCESTER, a smaller, paler, less rich cheese, is rarely made today.

LEICESTER

GREAT BRITAIN

A rich, russet colour, this is often labelled RED LEICESTER, but there is no other kind.

Leicester

It is smooth and firm, maturing at 3 months with a mellow flavour. The red colour comes from annatto dye.

WHITE STILTON

GREAT BRITAIN

This is a very young STILTON cheese which has not been allowed to develop any blue mould. Similar in texture to the regular, blue STILTON but much blander in flavour.

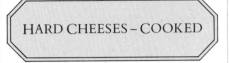

HARD CHEESES – COOKED

ALLGÄU EMMENTALER

GERMANY

This version of the famous Swiss cheese is a fine product in its own right. Hard and chewy with a slightly nutty flavour and plenty of cherry-sized holes, it too is made in large flat wheels. The Allgäu region in Bavaria where it is made is famous for its high-quality cheeses.

BERGKÄSE or ALPKÄSE is a similar cheese made exclusively in the high Alps.

BEAUFORT (GRUYERE DE BEAUFORT)

FRANCE

As the secondary name suggests, this is a Swiss-type cheese. It is made in large wheels with thin, natural rind and pale-yellow body with only a scattering of very small holes. It has a slightly higher fat content than others in the family, which gives it a mild, creamy flavour.

The cheese has been made in the Beaufort region of the Savoie mountains for many centuries, possibly even in Roman times, and its name is protected under French law.

Beaufort

COMTE (GRUYERE DE COMTE)

FRANCE

This French GRUYÈRE is closer to the Swiss original than BEAUFORT as it is scattered with hazelnut-sized holes. The body is smooth and golden, the flavour mellow. So

Comté

popular in France that it is not widely exported, COMTÉ is made in the same mountain region as Beaufort. The name is also legally protected.

EMMENTAL

SWITZERLAND

Known all over the world simply as Swiss cheese, EMMENTAL is widely imitated, with little success. Its incomparable qualities are due to the rich milk from cows that graze in Alpine meadows, and the skill of Swiss cheesemakers with centuries of experience. Originally it came from the valley *[tal]* of the River Emme; now it is made in almost all the German-speaking cantons of Switzerland. A genuine EMMENTAL has 'Switzerland' stamped on the top in concentric circles so that the word appears on every slice cut from the enormous flat wheels into which it is made. For export a single cheese must weigh at least 143 lb (64 kg) but the biggest wheels measure over 1 yd (1 m) across, and weigh more than 280 lb (125 kg).

Emmental

The famous holes, or eyes, the size of cherries, are evenly distributed through the ivory-coloured body. Drops of moisture or 'tears' in the eyes are a sign of a well-matured cheese. The dry, natural rind is brownish-yellow, with a faint sheen. Although the flavour is mild it is very subtle, often described as nutty.

GRUYERE

SWITZERLAND

Many people find this cheese hard to distinguish from EMMENTAL, and simply refer to them both as Swiss cheese. But GRUYÈRE is a smaller cheese, with only a few small holes scattered through it. Due to different treatment during a longer ripening period, the flavour is stronger, the texture slightly softer with a more yellow-amber body. The French-sounding name is

Gruyère

because it comes from the Gruyère district in the French-speaking part of Switzerland.

Like its big brother EMMENTAL, genuine GRUYÈRE is identified by the word Switzerland stamped all over it.

JARLSBERG

NORWAY

Jarlsberg

A cheese both old and new, as it was reinvented in the 1950s using an old recipe. In general appearance it is similar to EMMENTAL, with lots of round holes, but the actual cheese is softer, more like GOUDA, and the taste lies somewhere between the two. The name derives from a very old Norwegian estate.

GRANA PADANO

ITALY

Grana is the generic term for all hard, grainy cheeses produced in Italy. GRANA PADANO is the legally protected name of those produced by approved methods in a specific area. Basically, it is the same type of cheese as PARMESAN – but may be milder.

PARMESAN (PARMIGIANO-REGGIANI)

ITALY

Cheese sold as PARMESAN is found all over the world, but the real thing comes only from around the Parma and Reggio Emilia

areas in the Po valley. It is an extremely ancient cheese; records suggest it was made by the Etruscans, long before the Roman Empire.

The name, protected under Italian law, is stencilled into the rind of every cheese, and is a guarantee of superb quality. A whole one is a handsome sight: a big drum, with convex sides, weighing an average of 70 lb (30 kg). Most have a polished, old-gold rind though some are darker. The pale straw-coloured, grainy-textured interior, although hard, melts in the mouth. The flavour is delicate but unmistakable, with a characteristic aroma.

Genuine PARMESAN must be aged for at least a year, and much is left even longer – up to four years. A cheese marked STRAVECCHIO is three years old. Judged by weight, PARMESAN is a very expensive cheese; but a little goes a long way. To appreciate the true flavour and aroma, often entirely lacking from ready-grated (shredded) versions, buy a chunk, keep it out of the refrigerator and grate it when needed.

PARMESAN is made in several other countries, and in the United States the Stella brand from Wisconsin is well-regarded.

SBRINZ

SWITZERLAND

A hard grainy cheese, SBRINZ comes from the same family as the Italian grana cheeses such as PARMESAN. It is Switzerland's oldest cheese, and was being exported on mule-back over the St Gotthard Pass to Italy in the 15th century. The name comes from its village of origin, Brienz.

The cheese gets its strong character through long maturing: 18 months to two years. This gives it a hard, brittle texture and sharp, spicy flavour, making it ideal for grating and cooking. But young SBRINZ, known as SPALEN, is soft enough to eat as a dessert cheese. A whole cheese is a large chunky round, with a natural dry yellow-brown rind stamped with identifying marks.

CHAPTER THREE

SEMI-HARD CHEESES

emi-hard cheeses of the English type are produced in the same way as hard ones, but are more lightly pressed, or matured for a shorter time. Others are made in a variety of ways, the main difference being that the curd is not cheddared but gently heated or scalded, put straight into moulds and lightly pressed, then dipped in brine or dry-salted.

Semi-hard is a somewhat flexible definition, covering some cheese which might be called hard if marketed after a long ripening period, and others such as SAINT-PAULIN which have a buttery texture which makes them almost semi-soft.

Fat content of these cheeses is 40–50% in dry matter, unless otherwise stated.

APPENZELL

SWITZERLAND

First made in the Appenzell canton over 700 years ago, this is a delicate, tender cheese, which does not have the multiplicity of holes usually associated with Swiss cheese, just a few here and there. It is pale ivory-coloured with a yellowish-brown, slightly moist rind produced by washing it with wine or cider and spices. This gives the

Appenzell

cheese a pronounced spicy flavour. A whole cheese is a large flat wheel covered with a blue and gold label stamped with words and symbols identifying it as a genuine Swiss cheese.

BEL PAESE

ITALY

Bel Paese

Invented in the 1920s, this factory-made cheese is now popular all over the world, and is made in many other countries under licence. The original cheese, created by a member of the Galbani cheesemaking family, was modelled on SAINT-PAULIN, and it is very similar: a semi-soft supple cheese with a mild, almost sweet flavour, inside a shiny golden-yellow rind. BEL PAESE is most easily recognized by the wrapper, which bears a map of Italy and a portrait of an elderly cleric. He was the author of a children's book called *Bel Paese* (beautiful country), and a friend of Galbani's, who named the cheese both for him and their native country.

American-made BEL PAESE looks very similar at first glance, but the map on the wrapper shows North and South America.

BRICK

UNITED STATES

A genuine all-American cheese created in Wisconsin in 1877. Its inventor, John Jossi, was of Swiss descent, which may account for its holes and firm but soft texture. It is a cross between LIMBURGER and CHEDDAR. The flavour is mild and sweet when young, developing to quite pungent as it ages. It has a washed rind which can be smelly and bitter in a mature cheese, but this is

sometimes removed before it reaches the shops.

The name describes the shape, which is a modern block, though one story goes that it derives from the bricks originally used to press the cheese.

BUTTERKÄSE (DAMENKÄSE)

GERMANY

A very popular snack cheese in its homeland, this is smooth and soft as butter, hence the name. It is so bland and inoffensive it is also called 'ladies' cheese'. The body is pale yellow and slightly springy, without holes, the rind a thin reddish-gold. It is made in flat rounds or sausages.

CAERPHILLY

GREAT BRITAIN

The last remaining Welsh cheese, this is a relative newcomer, first made in about 1830 in a village near Cardiff – Caerphilly means 'castle town'. Today much of the cheese is made in England around

Caerphilly

Somerset. It is pure white, very moist and smooth, with a fresh, salty flavour and is eaten when only two weeks old.

EDAM

HOLLAND

The ball shape and red wax covering make this the most easily recognizable of all cheeses. However, to confuse the issue, in

Holland, EDAM has a natural yellow rind, and in the supermarket you may find it appearing in square or loaf shapes. But the cheese inside remains the same: ivory-coloured, smooth and springy, with a very few small holes. Most export EDAM is young – shipped at 4–5 weeks – so the flavour is mild.

MATURE EDAM (without red jacket) is stronger and drier. A regular ball of export

Edam

Edam weighs around 3½ lb (1.5 kg). BABY EDAMS weigh half that and make ideal whole cheeses to buy for a party. All are also available flavoured with cumin seeds.

Edam was first made in the town of that name about 600 years ago, and by the 17th century was already widely exported, mainly to the widely-scattered Dutch colonies. Nowadays it is all factory-made.

COMMISSIEKAAS is a double-sized, orange-coloured version known as MIMOLETTE in France.

ESROM

DENMARK

A brick-shaped supple cheese full of unevenly shaped holes, this is reminiscent of German TILSITER, especially if fully ripe and strong-smelling. The fat content is usually 45% but can be 60%. The yellowish-tan washed rind is milder than most and good to eat. The cheese, named after one made long ago by monks in the

Esrom

town of Esrom, is wrapped in red and gold foil for the export market.

FONTINA (FONTAL)

ITALY

Both these names derive from Mount Fontin in the Italian Alps. The first version can only be used for cheese produced in Valle d'Aosta, which is the original and higher-quality product. Other similar cheeses, produced in various parts of northern Italy and in France, must call themselves FONTAL.

Both cheeses are made in flattened drums, with a straw-coloured body scattered with small holes and a thin, rough, brownish-orange rind. Their flavour is mild and delicate; that of Fontina is superior because it is made from unpasteurized milk and matured longer.

GOUDA

HOLLAND

This is Holland's most important cheese and vast quantities are made every year, accounting for more than two-thirds of total Dutch cheese production. As nearly two-thirds of all Dutch cheese is exported, it's no wonder that GOUDA is one of the world's best-known cheeses. It is made all over Holland, in both factory and farmhouse. The name comes from the town of Gouda.

Although similar in texture and flavour to EDAM, GOUDA looks very different, being made in large, flattened wheels with a shiny, golden rind. It is also richer and creamier, as it has a higher fat content (48%). Most are sold young, at 4–8 weeks old; but there is also mature GOUDA, 8–12 weeks old and stronger-flavoured. Black-waxed GOUDA is even older – at least 17 weeks. FARMHOUSE GOUDA, made with unpasteurized milk, can be recognized by the word 'Boerenkaas' (farmer cheese) stamped into the rind.

Variations on the theme are BABY GOUDAS of varying weights; block GOUDA for speedy cutting; and GOUDA flavoured with cumin seeds, herbs or garlic.

Gouda

AMSTERDAM CHEESE is a version of Gouda with a higher moisture content, making it softer.

HANDKÄSE (HAND CHEESE)

GERMANY

These cheeses are so called because they were originally moulded by hand into small disc and roll shapes; farmhouse ones still are today. They were made by peasant farmers and their wives from very early times, using sour milk curds, and are sometimes known as SAUERMILCHKÄSE. They are very low in fat (under 10%). Genuine farmhouse specimens can be extremely pungent in both taste and smell, but factory-made, exported versions are likely to be milder.

HAND CHEESES have innumerable names describing their place of origin, and also vary in appearance. But HARZ and MAINZ, two of the best known, are easily recognized by their curious semi-translucent quality. The washed rind is ivory-white to golden-yellow, and perfectly edible; the body deep yellow and smooth-textured. MAINZ may take the form of a small roll, deeply indented into four or more portions.

HAND CHEESE is also made in the United States. German immigrants who settled in Pennsylvania took the recipe with them; it is now made throughout the Mid West. These cheeses have yellow to reddish-brown rinds and a soft creamy body; taste and smell become increasingly pungent as they continue to ripen.

HAVARTI

DENMARK

One of Denmark's best-known export cheeses, this is another version of the German TILSITER, similar to ESROM. It has the same creamy-white body full of irregular holes, but a milder flavour. Away from home it is most commonly seen in small blocks wrapped in blue and gold foil.

A richer version, with 60% fat content, has no rind, comes vacuum-packed in large blocks or smaller rounds and may be flavoured with caraway seeds.

The name Havarti is that of the farm belonging to Hanne Nielsen, a 19th-

Havarti

century Danish cheesemaker who started the revival of the now flourishing Danish cheese industry by copying well-known European cheeses.

LANCASHIRE

GREAT BRITAIN

This cheese is now made in two completely different versions which, unfortunately, look almost identical. FARMHOUSE

Lancashire

LANCASHIRE is a double curd cheese: the curd made from the evening milk is kept and added to the curd which is made the next morning. As this is a laborious and uneconomical process most factory-made LANCASHIRE is single curd. Both have a pale, almost white colour and crumbly texture; but the former has a creamy taste with a sharp tang to it, while the latter can only be described as bland, and is sometimes very dry.

LANCASHIRE is the cheese referred to by Ben Gunn in *Treasure Island* as 'Leigh Toaster' – it was once called that after the Lancashire village of Leigh where it originated.

MAASDAM

HOLLAND

A Dutch cheese that thinks it's Swiss – full of large holes. It is made in golden-rinded wheels similar to GOUDA, but the bacterial action which causes the holes also gives it a domed top.

MARIBO

DENMARK

This is similar to the SAMSOE cheeses but slightly more acidulous and flavourful. It is

Maríbo

usually seen as a large wheel with yellow paraffin wax coating, and may be flavoured with caraway seeds.

MOLBO

DENMARK

The Danish version of EDAM, it is ball-shaped, red-coated, firm and mild.

MONTEREY JACK (CALIFORNIA JACK, SONOMA JACK)

UNITED STATES

Technically a CHEDDAR, this cheese is eaten when so young – a mere two to three weeks – that it is very pale and extremely bland. At this stage it contains a lot of moisture, and is also known as HIGH MOISTURE JACK. A slightly different cheese, made from partly skimmed milk, is DRY or AGED JACK. This is matured for at least six months, and resembles a farmhouse CHEDDAR, with firm, deep-yellow body, dry, crusty rind and strong flavour. This version is a good grating cheese and so also known as GRATING-TYPE MONTEREY or JACK. Both are in blocks or wheels. JACK is often used as a substitute for the traditional cheeses in Mexican dishes.

SONOMA JACK is a special type of MONTEREY made by just two small firms in Sonoma County, California. The cheeses are cured in brine and turned by hand every day.

Monterey in California is the place where the cheese was first made in the 1840s. JACK comes from David Jacks who began marketing the cheese a little later. Even today the best JACK cheese comes from California, and variations such as dill-flavoured, jalapeño (chilli) or vegetarian JACK can only be obtained in the West.

MUROL

FRANCE

A cheese from the Auvergne region, with a firm texture and a mild flavour, it is always made with pasteurized milk. It's a large flattish disc with a central hole; so it is easily identifiable. The washed rind is light orange-brown, the body pale gold.

PORT-SALUT (PORT-DU-SALUT)

FRANCE

The combination of superbly smooth, springy-but-soft texture and mild but delicious flavour have made this an enduringly popular cheese. It is made in small flat cylinders; the body is pale yellow, the rind deep orange. Although it has a washed rind, it lacks the strong smell associated with many such cheeses, but

Port-Salut

retains the extra tang obtained by the process. It is a genuine monastery cheese with a rather complicated history.

It was first made by Trappist monks in the early 19th century and named after their abbey. When they marketed the cheese it became so successful that it was widely copied, and in 1938 the trade name PORT-SALUT was registered for cheeses made at the abbey. After World War II they sold the trade name, and PORT-SALUT became a factory-made cheese. But the monks continued to make the cheese at the abbey, and this is now known as ENTRAMMES, the name of the town where it stands. (See also SAINT-PAULIN.)

PYRENEES CHEESE

FRANCE

A distinctive-looking but mild-flavoured cheese with a shiny black, waxed rind. It

Pyrénées Cheese

comes in chunky drums and the pale, straw-coloured, springy body is full of small holes.

RACLETTE

SWITZERLAND

This is not one cheese, but a whole group of cheeses, all suitable for making the traditional Swiss dish *raclette*. The word means 'scraper', and making the dish involves melting a cut side of cheese in front of an open fire and scraping the

Raclette

melted portion on to potatoes boiled in their jackets. RACLETTE cheeses are also good table cheeses.

The best-known RACLETTES originally came from the Canton of Valais, but they are now made all over Switzerland. Like most Swiss cheeses they are made in large flat wheels, but have only a scattering of holes. The body is pale yellow, the rind rough and greyish-brown and the flavour is similar to GRUYÈRE.

ROYALP

SWITZERLAND

Once known as SWISS TILSIT, this is a relatively modern cheese, having been introduced by German cheesemakers in the

Royalp

last century. It is actually much milder than TILSITER, but stronger than APPENZELL, which it closely resembles in appearance.

SAINT-NECTAIRE

FRANCE

Made in the Auvergne region since the Middle Ages, this is a great cheese with a protected name. It comes in flat wheels

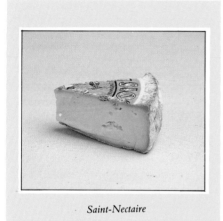

Saint-Nectaire

weighing 2–3 lbs (1–1.5 kg). Long maturing in damp cellars gives the natural dry rind a spectacular red, yellow and white mould growth. The cheese inside is pale yellow, and should have a mild but exquisite flavour. This is sometimes absent if the cheese has been made with pasteurized milk. The best indication of a raw-milk SAINT-NECTAIRE is an oval stamp indicating that it is farmhouse-made (factory ones have rectangular stamps) but this is not a complete guarantee of authenticity.

SAINT-PAULIN

FRANCE

This is the name used for versions of PORT-SALUT made in factories all over France. It is only ripened for two to three weeks; so it is very mild. It comes in 8-in (20-cm) rounds, with a bright orange washed rind. The body is creamy-yellow and very smooth and soft.

Saint-Paulin

SAMSOE

DENMARK

Although it looks rather like a Swiss cheese, being made in a big wheel with a few holes in it, SAMSOE has a firm, sliceable, Cheddar-like consistency. As with CHEDDAR it is the country's favourite cheese, and is mild or full-flavoured depending on its age when eaten. The name is that of one of Denmark's many islands.

Also like CHEDDAR, SAMSOE is the head of a family of similar cheeses: DANBO, ELBO, FYNBO and TYBO. These all vary in shape and size, and the finish can be paraffin wax yellow like SAMSOE, or red like EDAM.

Samsoe

In general DANBO is a flat square, ELBO and TYBO block-shaped and FYNBO a small wheel. DANBO and TYBO may be flavoured with caraway seeds.

TETE DE MOINE (BELLELAY)

SWITZERLAND

Made in small, tall cylinders, this is called 'monk's head' because when a horizontal slice is removed from the top the pale body, encircled by reddish-brown rind, resembles

Tête de Moine

a monk's tonsure. It is also a monastery cheese, first made at Bellelay Abbey as long as 800 years ago. The spicy, aromatic flavour is best released by paring off curls of cheese with a sharp knife or cheese-slice. It comes wrapped in foil.

TILSITER

GERMANY

First made by Dutchmen living in the town of Tilsit in East Prussia (now part of the Soviet Union), this is one of those cheeses claimed to have been the result of a happy

Tilsiter

accident. Cheeses supposed to turn out as GOUDA were stored in a damp place which caused them to mature in a completely different way, producing the soft texture and multiplicity of cracks or oval holes characteristic of the cheese we know today. Modern TILSITER can be rather unlike its ancestor: the original was made in large wheels, but today is likely to be a block; and the washed rind, which gives it a pronounced aroma and pungent flavour, may have been removed before it reaches you. Fat content ranges from 30–50%.

TOMME (TOME) DE SAVOIE

FRANCE

The name simply means cheese of Savoy, and refers to any of the cheeses made in that mountainous region of south-eastern France. Genuine TOMMES are thick wheels with grey or brown, dry powdery natural rinds; copies often have a black plastic coat. The body is firm, smooth and pale yellow with a mild flavour.

There are several local variants and one which is flavoured with fennel. Although usually made from skimmed cow's milk, TOMME is frequently made from goat's milk, when it is called TOMME DE CHÊVRE. TOMME AUX RAISINS should be a version of this cheese coated with grape skins and pips left over after wine-making. But the name

Tomme de Savoie

is often used for a processed cheese covered with black wax and dried grape pips, which is properly called FONDU AUX RAISINS or Grape Cheese.

Vacherin Fribourgeois

VACHERIN FRIBOURGEOIS

SWITZERLAND

One of the oldest Swiss cheeses; the name means, made by the herdsmen *(vaccarinus)* of the Canton of Fribourg. It is a typical Swiss cheese, made in large flat wheels, but has no holes, just a lot of small cracks. The texture is smooth, the taste delicate and creamy.

WENSLEYDALE

GREAT BRITAIN

Although it has been made in the Yorkshire Dales for over a thousand years, WENSLEYDALE was originally a French cheese, made by monks who came to England with William the Conqueror. Their cheese was more like the ROQUEFORT they knew back home, being made from sheep's milk, and blue-veined. Gradually cow's milk replaced sheep's, but right up until the 1920s it remained blue. Today WENSLEYDALE is virtually all white, and the blue is a rarity.

WHITE WENSLEYDALE is eaten when only three weeks old; so it is mild and moist. The texture is pleasantly crumbly. BLUE WENSLEYDALE is matured for longer – six months – and has a richer almost sweet taste.

SOFT RIPENED CHEESES

This group of cheeses consists of those which are unpressed, and therefore very soft, and which are ripened for anything from a few days to several weeks or more. The softness of the cheese depends on how much of the whey is extracted and how long it is ripened. There are two distinct types, those with bloomy or flowery rinds, and those with washed rinds.

A bloomy rind is produced by spraying the cheese with the mould *Penicillium candidum,* to encourage speedy blooming of a dry, velvety mould which formerly occurred naturally but slowly. On a young cheese this rind is soft, white and perfectly edible, but as the cheese ages, it becomes darker, harder and increasingly less palatable. Ripening takes place from the outside inwards; if there is a white chalky centre the cheese is not fully mature. With a farmhouse cheese, ripening continues so that within a few days it becomes runny. But many factory-made ones are stabilized and supplied in medium-ripe condition. They will not mature any further, but dry out unpleasantly.

Washed rind cheeses are so called because they are washed during the ripening period with any one of a variety of liquids – wine, beer, water, brine or a diluted bacterial culture. This encourages the growth of coryne bacteria which make the rind yellow to dark orange in colour, moist and sometimes very pungent. Such rinds are too strong for most people's taste.

The fat content of most soft ripened cheeses lies in the 40–50% range, though a few, particularly recent introductions are double or triple cream with 60–75% fat.

BLOOMY RIND CHEESES

BOURSAULT

FRANCE

A popular triple cream cheese which is

Boursault

superbly mellow and rich, with a delicate rind. It comes in small wrapped cylinders. Named after its inventor, it is factory-made in northern France.

BRIE

FRANCE

Probably the most famous French cheese next to CAMEMBERT, BRIE has a long history and was being made at least as far back as the 13th century. It is named after the district of La Brie, along the Marne Valley near Paris. A whole BRIE is a large flat disc, packed in a chipwood box and labelled to show its origin. Prepacked portions come in triangular boxes. The body of a perfect cheese is smooth and satiny, almost bursting out of the snowy rind, and once cut it tends to overflow. If the cheese has a chalky centre it is too

Brie de Meaux

young; if it is liquifying it is too old. The flavour ranges from mild to strong depending on the type of BRIE and how long it has been ripened. Most BRIE nowadays is factory-made, from pasteurized milk, and if it's not stamped 'Made in France' it wasn't.

BRIE DE MEAUX and BRIE DE MELUN are protected names *(appellation contrôlée)* for BRIE cheeses made according to strict rules

Petit Brie 60

in their respective areas. BRIE DE MEAUX was elected King of Cheeses at a contest held during the Congress of Vienna in 1815. Both are connoisseur's cheeses, and well ripened. This gives them a richer flavour than other BRIES, and a darker rind dappled with a reddish-brown colour.

In recent years, several new types of BRIE with a higher fat content – 60% – have been introduced. Brand names include LE CREMEUX, PETIT BRIE 60 and BRIE HAUTE MARQUE.

BRILLAT-SAVARIN

FRANCE

A triple-cream cheese, popular for dessert, from Normandy, named after the famous French gourmet. It has a dazzling white rind and body and is made in medium-and large-sized rounds.

CAMEMBERT

FRANCE

This is one of the world's great cheeses, and accounts for around 20 % of all the

Camembert

hundreds of cheeses produced in France. The credit for creating Camembert goes to an 18th-century Normandy farmer's wife named Marie Harel. Although probably not the original inventor, she was known as a superb cheesemaker, and her cheeses, named after the village of Camembert, became so famous that two statues and an obelisk have been erected in her memory.

Mme. Harel's CAMEMBERT didn't look much like modern ones. It had no snowy white rind, but often turned out blue, and did not come in the familiar round box – that was only introduced in the 1890s. Otherwise it was the same – a small round cheese, no more than 4 in (10 cm) across, with a soft rind encasing a pale golden body. Nowadays it is also sold in halves and portion-sized wedges. A perfectly ripe CAMEMBERT should fit its box perfectly, without appearing too loose or too tight a fit; the rind should be soft enough to yield to gentle finger pressure, with no raised edge. The flavour should be rich and creamy, reminiscent of BRIE but with more tang to it. Although CAMEMBERT is made in much the same way, its different size affects the surface ripening process and alters the taste.

CAMEMBERT is so popular that it is now made all over the world, and some truly horrible or totally tasteless cheese masquerades under this name; some CAMEMBERT is even sold in cans! Most CAMEMBERT is factory-made, often a long way from France, and can be good, if

blander than the original. But the very best still comes from Normandy and is sold under the protected name CAMEMBERT DE NORMANDIE. The initials VCN on a label stand for *Véritable Camembert de Normandie*.

CAPRICE DES DIEUX

FRANCE

Caprice des Dieux

A small oval double-cream cheese sold in cardboard boxes, with an interesting but mild flavour. The name means 'whim-of-the-Gods'.

CARRE DE L'EST

FRANCE

A small square cheese from north-eastern France, whose name means 'square of the

Carré de l'Est

east'. It is produced by the same process as CAMEMBERT, but is milder and slightly salted.

CHAOURCE

FRANCE

Chaource

This too is similar to CAMEMBERT, but smaller and taller. The name (from the village where it was originally made) is protected, and applies only to cheeses made by the approved method in the Champagne region.

Coulommiers

COULOMMIERS (PETIT BRIE)

FRANCE

BRIE's baby brother is a smaller but thicker cheese and looks more like CAMEMBERT. Otherwise it is very like BRIE, but milder in flavour as it is generally eaten when very young.

EXCELSIOR

FRANCE

Rich, and creamy (72% fat) this is a cheese from Normandy with a delicate white rind and ivory body, sold in small log shapes. It was first made in the 1890s when its mild flavour made it popular as a breakfast cheese.

EXPLORATEUR

FRANCE

Explorateur

A similar cheese to EXCELSIOR, but even richer – 75% fat, triple-cream – and is made in the Ile de France region near Paris.

MELBURY

GREAT BRITAIN

The British BRIE: a recent introduction with mild, soft interior and white surface mould. It is made in small blocks and wrapped in golden foil.

NEUFCHATEL

FRANCE

This famous creamy-white, very smooth soft cheese is almost fresh, as it is ripened for such a short time that the white rind flora can only just be seen. It is named after the French town of Neufchâtel in the Pays de Bray on the northern coast. In France it is slightly salty; the American version is sweeter. It is a small cheese and comes in a

Neufchâtel

number of different shapes, the best known of which are BONDON (bung-shaped) and COEUR DE BRAY (heart-shaped).

NEUFCHÂTEL AFFINÉ is a longer-ripened version; FOURNAY AFFINÉ is a similar cheese from a neighbouring area.

TELEME

UNITED STATES

A soft cheese found mainly in northern California, it is modelled on American-made BRIE but with more flavour.

TOMME BLANCHE

FRANCE

Tomme Blanche

The general name for soft buttery cheeses made in fairly large thick rounds. Look for: BELLE NORMANDE, CHAMOIS D'OR, DOUCEUR D'AUVERGNE and VIGNOLAS.

VIGNOTTE

FRANCE

A relatively new cheese, rather firmer than most that are classified as soft. Made in medium-sized thick rounds, it is very rich and creamy (72% fat) with a sharp tang.

Vignotte

WASHED RIND CHEESES

BRAND-NAME CHEESES

FRANCE

A large number of soft cheeses with creamy, springy interiors, usually sprinkled with holes and with shiny golden rinds, are exported from France under various brand names. They are generally mild in flavour with a slight tang, and made in medium-

Belle des Champs

Chaumes

Saint-Albray

Gormelin

Vacherol

Pont Moutier

sized flattened rounds. Some are well established, some quite new. Look for: BELLE DES CHAMPS, CHAUMES, DRAKKAR, GORMELIN, LE PAILLERON, PONT MOUTIER, ROND NORMAND, SAINT ALBRAY, VACHEROL and VIEUX PANÉ.

EPOISSES

FRANCE

This very soft-textured cheese from Burgundy with strong tangy flavour and penetrating aroma is made in small fat

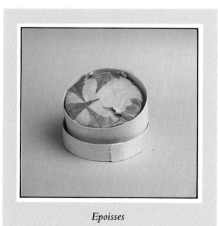

Epoisses

disks. The deep orange, matt rind is washed with brandy and is very delicious. EPOISSES also comes flavoured with black pepper, fennel or cloves.

HERVE

BELGIUM

A family of strong-smelling cheeses from around the town of Herve in Liège. Made in small squares, 3 in (8 cm) thick, the cheeses are supple and pale yellow under the reddish-brown rind. The best-known HERVE cheese is REMOUDOU.

LIEDERKRANZ

UNITED STATES

This is one of the few American originals, developed by a cheesemaker called Emil Frey in New York in 1892. He was trying to imitate a German cheese called SCHLOSSKÄSE, but ended up with something more like a milder and less pungent form of LIMBURGER. He tried it out on a singing group of fellow immigrants to which he belonged; they approved, so he named it after them – *liederkranz* means 'song circle'. It has a pale-brown rind and is soft ivory inside. Nowadays LIEDERKRANZ is marketed in foil-wrapped 4-oz (115-g) bars by Borden of Ohio. These are date-stamped so that consumers can eat the cheese when young and mild, or leave it to develop its full flavour.

LIMBURGER

GERMANY

Originally this was a Belgian cheese, but production was taken up by cheesemakers in the Allgäu region of south Germany in the 19th century, and abandoned in Belgium. It is made in blocks of varying size, and is famous for the pungent smell of the soft, slightly wrinkled, yellow-brown rind. The cheese itself is pale yellow, soft and quite mild. Regarded by many cheesemakers as the most difficult and delicate cheese to produce, it is made in several different grades with a fat content

Limburger

ranging from 20–50% which is indicated on the foil wrapping. LIMBURGER is also made in the United States and is especially popular in areas where large numbers of Germans settled.

LIVAROT

FRANCE

One of the great cheeses originating from the Pays d'Auge region of Normandy. Not for the fainthearted, it has an overpowering smell, which fortunately disappears once the orange-brown rind is removed. The

Livarot

cheese inside is springy, golden and surprisingly mild, with a scattering of small holes. It is round and flat, like a CAMEMBERT, but larger.

LIVAROT (named after the town) is one of France's oldest cheeses, and the name is protected. A genuine one bears the legend *Fabriqué dans le Pays d'Auge* on the box.

MAROILLES

FRANCE

The classic example of a 'monastery cheese', as it was invented by a monk in the abbey of Maroilles, near Lille in Flanders, during the 10th century. When fully ripe it

Maroilles

smells so fearsomely that it is nicknamed *Vieux Puant* (Old Stinker). Although not to everyone's taste, it is one of France's greatest cheeses, and the name is protected by law.

The moist, shiny, reddish rind is produced by brine-washing throughout a long ripening period of four to six months. The body is soft and pale yellow and the flavour strong but never sharp. In shape, the cheese is a thick square produced in a range of weights from 1¾ lb (800 g) down to only 7 oz (200 g).

MUNSTER (MÜNSTER, MUENSTER)

FRANCE, GERMANY

MUNSTER was first made in the Middle Ages, allegedly by Irish monks settled in the Munster valley of Alsace Lorraine.

Now largely a region of France, Alsace has changed from a German to a French province and vice versa several times over the last few centuries; so it is not surprising that it is made in Germany too, where it is known as MÜNSTER. It is a typical 'monastery' cheese, consisting of small, fat

Munster

discs with orange rinds and a rich, yellow body. The taste should be tangy and full, but although MUNSTER is a protected name the cheese is widely copied, and imitations are often bland. Check the label for the key words 'Alsace-Lorraine' or 'Vosges'. A Munster-style cheese is also produced in the United States where it is usually referred to as MUENSTER.

MUNSTER GÉRÔMÉ is a similar cheese but bigger.

PONT L'EVEQUE

FRANCE

Along with CAMEMBERT and LIVAROT, this is one of the three world-renowned cheeses from the Pays d'Auge in Normandy. It has been made since the Middle Ages, but in the 17th century it was renamed after the town in Calvados which was its main

Pont l'Evêque

market. Previously it was called ANGELOT. Made in small, shallow squares, it has a deep yellow rind and a soft golden-yellow inside. When perfectly ripe it has a strong smell and taste; but if it has an acrid smell and bitter taste it is overripe. The name is protected and its box should state its Normandy origin.

REBLOCHON

FRANCE

This cheese gets its name from the local Savoyard word meaning to milk for a second time – originally it was made by the herdsmen for their own use with milk

Reblochon

smuggled out of the cows after the farmer thought they had finished milking for the day. Ironically, because it ripens rapidly and is unpleasantly bitter when overripe, it is now a fairly rare and expensive cheese. The name is protected.

It takes the form of a flattened round, either 5 or 8 in (13 or 20 cm) across, which is usually packed between thin wooden disks. The rind is a matt pinkish-grey and the body creamy and pale with a rich flavour.

REMOUDOU

BELGIUM

The most famous of the HERVE cheese family, it is ripened for longer than most, ending up with a dark, orange-brown rind that smells more powerfully even than a LIMBURGER. This has earnt it the name of 'the stinking cheese'. Its name comes from the Walloon word *remoud,* meaning the extra-rich milk cows give at the end of their lactation period.

The body is soft and buttery, and tastes similar to LIMBURGER. It is cut into small cubes, and a factory-made one may be rindless and plastic wrapped. Some are described as double cream, although the fat content is only 45–52%.

ROMADUR

GERMANY

A soft, milder version of LIMBURGER, more like the American LIEDERKRANZ. Made in various grades; fat content 20–60%.

TALEGGIO

ITALY

One of Italy's few soft ripened cheeses, produced in the small town of that name and throughout Lombardy since the 11th century. It comes in big square blocks with a thin, soft, pink or greyish rind. The body is off-white and the taste mild.

Taleggio

CHAPTER FIVE

BLUE-VEINED CHEESES

This group of cheeses originated accidentally when unhygienic storage conditions led to the development of blue moulds inside the ripening cheese. It was very soon discovered that far from being inedible, mouldy cheeses were delicious. Cheesemakers learnt how to encourage the mould growth by storing the cheese in limestone cellars or caves where the bacteria occurred naturally.

Nowadays the process is more scientific. The blueing is achieved by sprinkling a mould preparation on the curds, and skewering holes into the ripening cheese to form air passages for the mould to grow in. ROQUEFORT and STILTON are made with *Pencillium roqueforti;* GORGONZOLA with *Penicillium glaucum.*

Traditional blue cheeses are very strongly flavoured and fairly firm in texture with fat content in the 45–50% range. However, some recently introduced varieties are much milder, softer and richer.

AMERICAN BLUE

UNITED STATES

Based on ROQUEFORT, but using cow's milk, AMERICAN BLUE cheeses produced by the big manufacturers are semi-hard, strong and salty, all right for cooking, crumbling into salads and adding to salad dressings, but not the equal of even the humbler European blues as table cheeses. Some of the blue cheeses produced by smaller companies are excellent, each with its own character. A few of the better brands are MAYTAG BLUE, MINNESOTA BLUE, NAUVOO and OREGON BLUE. However, these cheeses are hard to find outside their own areas.

BELLE BRESSANE

FRANCE

One of the more modern, soft blue cheeses with fairly mild flavour, from the region of Bresse. Easily identified – it is a large flat cake with a hole in the middle.

BLEU D'AUVERGNE

FRANCE

Originally created in the last century as an imitation of ROQUEFORT using cow's milk instead of sheep's, this is now a respected cheese in its own right, and the name is protected. It is semi-hard and made in chunky cylinders weighing 5½–10 lb (2.5–4.5 kg), wrapped in foil encircled with a

Bleu d'Auvergne

green band and stamped to show that they come from the Auvergne. Like ROQUEFORT, BLEU D'AUVERGNE has no rind, just a very thin skin. The flavour is full without being too strong. It may not compare with ROQUEFORT but is much more affordable.

BLEU DE BRESSE

FRANCE

Bleu de Bresse

During World War II very little GORGONZOLA was imported into France, and a large cheese called SAINGORLON was made to fill the gap. In the 1950s a smaller version was introduced, and became established as a cheese in its own right under the name BLEU DE BRESSE. It is made in slim cylinders and when young it has the consistency of very stiffly whipped cream. The flavour should be fairly mild for a blue cheese; if it is strong and salty, it is overripe.

BLUE BRIE

DENMARK, FRANCE, GERMANY

Bavarian Blue

This is a recently invented soft cheese sold under various brand names, including BAVARIAN BLUE, CAMBAZOLA, SAGA BLUE, OPUS 84. Although they have the white bloomy rind of a BRIE they are much richer, because added cream gives them a 60–70% fat content. They are made in the traditional large flat rounds and also in other shapes. The blueing is in the form of patches rather than veins. See also LYMESWOLD.

BLUE CASTELLO

DENMARK

A variation on BLUE BRIE – this has no bloomy white rind, and the blueing may take the form of horizontal strips. A fat content of 70% makes it very mild and creamy. If it is exceptionally well-ripened,

Blue Castello

a yellow to reddish-brown rind may develop. It is sold in blue-and-white boxes.

BLUE CHESHIRE

GREAT BRITAIN

As it is the 'red', anatto-dyed version of CHESHIRE cheese which is blued, it is quite a startling sight – a deep marigold colour

Blue Cheshire

richly veined with blue. The flavour is very distinctive as the cheese is already salty and the blueing adds an extra tang. However, it is a rare and expensive cheese.

BLUE CREME

DENMARK

An ingot-shaped bar of soft mild white cheese layered with two strips of DANISH BLUE, this is a pale shadow of Italian TORTA.

BLUE WENSLEYDALE

GREAT BRITAIN

In the past WENSLEYDALE was always a blue cheese, but today the blued version is very

Blue Wensleydale

rare. The blueing, plus a longer maturing time of six months, gives it a fine mellow flavour.

DANISH BLUE (DANABLU)

DENMARK

This cheese was developed this century as a substitute ROQUEFORT, using cow's milk. It didn't turn out anything like the model –

Danish Blue (Danablu)

it is white and crumbly, with a sharp, salty taste. But it appeals to those who like strong flavours, and has the great virtue of being inexpensive. It is made in large drums or blocks and has no rind.

DOLCE LATTE

ITALY

Dolce Latte

The registered brand name of a factory-made GORGONZOLA. It is exceptionally creamy and mild – the name means 'sweet milk'.

DORSET BLUE (BLUE VINNEY)

GREAT BRITAIN

BLUE VINNEY as such is an extinct cheese. It was a very hard, white-bodied blue made in Dorset when ideas about hygiene were so primitive that tales that the blueing was achieved by dipping mouldy harness leather into the milk are quite believable. The name Vinney comes from the Old English word for mould, *fyniz*. Improved hygiene, plus changing tastes, killed it off,

Dorset Blue (Blue Vinney)

but interest in it survives. For some years unscrupulous merchants satisfied the demand for BLUE VINNEY with second-grade STILTON. But now a farmhouse producer in Dorset is making the real thing in limited quantities.

EDELPILZKÄSE(PILZKÄSE)

GERMANY

Very pale, almost white cheese with blue-green veins and piquant flavour. It is quite crumbly, yet sliceable, and made in drums or loaves. The full name means 'noble mould cheese' – *pilze* being a colloquial term for moulds and fungi.

FOURME D'AMBERT

FRANCE

This is somewhat similar in flavour to ROQUEFORT, but with a rough reddish-yellow rind that resembles GORGONZOLA.

Fourme d'Ambert

In appearance it is similar to a baby STILTON, being a tall cylinder weighing 4 pounds (1.75 kg). The word *fourme* denotes a cheese from the mountains of the Auvergne, where Ambert is located. It is also known as FOURME DE MONTBRISON; both names are protected.

GORGONZOLA

ITALY

An ancient cheese known to have been made for over a thousand years,

Gorgonzola

GORGONZOLA is popular today all over the world for its imcomparable flavour and creamy texture – it is one of the mildest of blue cheeses. A perfect piece should be dense and soft, pale straw-coloured, with greeny-blue flecks throughout, and have a rough reddish rind. GORGONZOLA was originally one of the STRACCHINO-type cheeses, produced during the winter in the Parish of Gorgonzola in Lombardy. Today it is made all year round in many parts of the world, but true GORGONZOLA still comes only from Lombardy. It is made in thick wheels measuring up to a foot across, wrapped in foil stamped all over with the letter 'g' or other official markings.

LYMESWOLD

GREAT BRITAIN

Lymeswold

Recently-introduced soft cheese with blue veining and white surface mould. Similar to BLUE BRIE but slightly firmer.

MELLOW BLUE

DENMARK

Second cousin to DANISH BLUE but smoother in texture, it has a milder flavour which is achieved by higher fat content – 60%.

MYCELLA

DENMARK

The Danish version of GORGONZOLA: a fairly soft, creamy-white cheese with greeny-blue veining and soft whitish-

Mycella

brown rind. It is milder and smoother than either DANISH BLUE or MELLOW BLUE. Named for the variety of mould called *mycella* used to make it, it is moulded in large drums or blocks.

PIPOCREM

FRANCE

A mild semi-soft blue cheese, made in logs of varying sizes with a white rind, it is produced in the Ile de France region.

ROQUEFORT

FRANCE

The *crème de la crème* of blue cheeses, ROQUEFORT is made from sheep's milk,

Roquefort

Stilton

which gives it a unique flavour and smooth creamy texture. It is also one of the oldest of the world's cheeses, known to have existed at least 2000 years ago, when it was mentioned in glowing terms by the Roman writer Pliny.

ROQUEFORT was originally made in a village called Roquefort-sur-Soulzon situated on top of a network of limestone caves – the now-famous caves of Combalou. It is said to have been discovered when a herdsman left his lunch of bread and curd cheese inside one of these, returning a week later to find the cheese transformed by greeny-blue mould; fortunately for us he was brave enough to taste it. Be that as it may, the conditions inside the caves – plenty of natural ventilation and a moist, cool atmosphere – create a unique cheese which cannot be duplicated anywhere else.

As far back as 1411, the cheesemakers persuaded Charles VI to grant them sole rights to the name, and it has been strictly protected ever since. Although demand for ROQUEFORT is now so great that it is made as far away as the island of Corsica, it must all be ripened in the Combalou caves. The chunky cylinders are wrapped in foil

towards the end of their ripening and stamped with the red sheep emblem, which is the guarantee of a genuine ROQUEFORT.

This wrapping produces a cheese with almost no detectable rind. The flavour should be full yet subtle, with no trace of harshness. Unfortunately, exported ROQUEFORT is sometimes oversalted so that it will keep longer.

SHROPSHIRE BLUE

GREAT BRITAIN

Shropshire Blue

Despite its name, this originated in Scotland in the 1970s, and is now made in Leicestershire in small quantities. It resembles BLUE CHESHIRE in being orange-coloured with blue veining, but is softer.

STILTON

GREAT BRITAIN

'The King of English cheeses' is produced exclusively by a handful of dairy companies in Leicestershire, Nottinghamshire and Derbyshire, from where it is exported all over the world. The name is a protected trade mark.

STILTON is known to have existed by the earth 18th century, and is unusual for a British cheese in being named after a town. Its fame began to spread after it was served to stage-coach travellers when they stopped at the Bell Inn at Stilton in Cambridgeshire. However, the cheese was never made there, but was supplied by Leicestershire farmers.

Although STILTON is not pressed, it is a semi-hard cheese, with a crusty greyish-brown rind dusted with white. It is made in tall cylinders, in varying weights ranging from 4–18 lb (2–8 kg). The blue veins radiate out from the centre, and the body should be a rich creamy colour, like old piano keys. The flavour is full-bodied and tangy, never sharp unless the cheese is underripe.

TORTA

ITALY

The word means cake in Italian and refers to a luxurious cheese layer cake – a combination of fresh cheese, usually MASCARPONE, layered with GORGONZOLA. Nuts, olives or caraway seeds may also be included. Very rich with 60% fat, TORTAS come block shaped and foil-wrapped.

CHAPTER SIX

*F*RESH *C*HEESES

his is the family of soft white cheeses which are ready to eat as soon as they are made, or after just a few days' ripening, before any rind has developed. Most are so soft they are packed in containers and are spoonable; some are moulded or lightly pressed to make them firm enough to keep their shape and be sliced. All owe their softness to a high moisture content – 60–80%. Flavour is mild and slightly acidic.

CURD OR LACTIC CHEESES

All types of unripened soft cheeses are described as curd or lactic cheeses.

The simplest kind of fresh cheese is produced by allowing milk to sour naturally and separate into curds and whey, then draining off the whey. These are called lactic-curd or acid-curd cheeses. The finest, most delicately flavoured fresh cheeses are produced in this way.

In large-scale manufacture, the milk may be heat-treated, to destroy possibly harmful bacteria. This may also kill the bacteria responsible for coagulation; so a bacterial starter culture is used, usually with a small amount of rennet to help the curd form. Sometimes rennet alone is used. Rennet-curd cheeses have a different texture and flavour from acid-curd ones.

Further variations are obtained by cutting and heating the curd to develop the desired texture. Salt is sometimes added, plus any flavourings such as chopped vegetables or herbs.

These methods produce a wide range of soft fresh cheeses of varying flavour and texture. The fat content also varies, according to whether skimmed milk or full-cream milk is used, and whether any cream is added. Different countries have their own regulations regarding the description of fat content.

COTTAGE CHEESES

In the past, when country people owned or kept milking animals and made their own butter, they used the skimmed milk left behind to make simple acid-curd 'cottage' cheeses. The cottage cheeses of today are made in huge vats in cheese factories by the American washed and creamed curd process which produces a rather different cheese – granular instead of smooth, with a higher water content. The skimmed-milk curds are heated and agitated, then washed several times in chilled water and cooled. The washing reduces the acidity of the curd and also removes the whey. After draining, the curd is blended with salted cream; a stabilizer is often added as well.

Depending on how much cream is added to the skimmed milk, cottage cheeses have a fat content of around 4%.

CREAM CHEESES

These are made by using cream of varying fat contents, and processing it in a slightly different way from curd cheese to produce a soft buttery texture. After draining, the curd is mixed with preservatives, stabilizers, salt and sometimes flavourings and then cooked. This makes it firm enough to mould into small cylinders, squares or other shapes. When cool it is packed in a light-excluding wrapping, such as aluminium foil, in order to keep it fresh.

Regulations concerning minimum fat content vary slightly from country to country. In Great Britain cream cheese must have at least 45%; double cream 65%. In the United States the figures are 35% and 60%. Triple-cream cheeses contain 75%.

BAKERS' CHEESE

UNITED STATES

An extra-moist, sour, low-fat cottage cheese with fine granules, used to make cheese pastry.

BOURSIN

FRANCE

An extremely popular, near triple-cream cheese (70–75% fat), packed in low cylinders or small boxes. It can be flavoured with herbs, garlic or crushed black peppercorns. The word *gournay* on the wrapper refers to its origins; it is a factory-

Boursin

made, unripened form of a small CAMEMBERT made at Gournay in Normandy.

CABOC

GREAT BRITAIN

A recent revival of a 15th-century Scottish double-cream cheese covered in oatmeal and made in small cylinders. It has a fairly bland flavour.

COTTAGE CHEESE

GREAT BRITAIN

By far the most popular soft cheese in weight-conscious Great Britain; sales have increased twelvefold over the last 15 or so

Cottage Cheese

years. It is the wet, granular American type. Plain COTTAGE CHEESE is very bland; so versions flavoured with chives, onion and peppers, pineapple or CHEDDAR have been developed. All are packed in cartons.

COTTAGE CHEESE

UNITED STATES

In America COTTAGE CHEESE is the next in popularity to CHEDDAR, and consumption per head is nine times greater than that for Great Britain. Most widely available of the many varieties is sweet-curd COTTAGE CHEESE, but an acid-curd version, with a more tangy flavour, is also made. This used to be known as New York or country style. CREAMED COTTAGE CHEESE contains 4% cream, bringing the fat content up to 8%. All sorts of different flavourings are added, and the texture of the cheese varies according to brand. Some are granular (California style), others are whipped (pot style).

CREAM CHEESE

GREAT BRITAIN

British CREAM CHEESES are usually labelled full fat soft cheese, and can be single or double cream. They are sometimes sold by

Cream Cheese

weight, but more often come packed in small foil-wrapped portions or tubs, plain or with added flavourings.

CREAM CHEESE

UNITED STATES

American CREAM CHEESE can be quite firm, appearing in large wrapped bricks, or whipped until softer and packed in waxed cartons. Its flavour is fresh with a sour tang. CREAM CHEESE and jelly (jam) is an established favourite for sandwiches.

American NEUFCHÂTEL, copied from the original French version, is eaten unripened, before it has a chance to develop any bloomy white rind. It is like CREAM CHEESE but more moist, and may be flavoured with fruit, vegetables, herbs or spices.

DEMI-SEL

FRANCE

A well-known rennet-curd cheese which is moulded into small flat squares and packed in foil. The name comes from its being semi-salted; fat content is 40%. GERVAIS is a popular brand.

FARMER CHEESE

UNITED STATES

This is COTTAGE CHEESE pressed into the shape of a brick. In some parts of the United States it is eaten for breakfast with fruit and sour cream. It is also used in cooking.

FONTAINEBLEU

FRANCE

An extremely light, unsalted double-CREAM CHEESE similar to PETIT-SUISSE, usually eaten as a dessert with fruit and sugar.

FROMAGE BLANC

FRANCE

The skimmed-milk form of this rennet-curd cheese is fat-free, and has become popular along with *nouvelle cuisine* and *cuisine minceur*. But in Great Britain it is not widely available outside London.

FROMAGE FRAIS

FRANCE

The French term for fresh unripened white cheeses, of varying consistency and fat contents ranging from 40–60%. There are triple-cream cheeses with 75% fat content. Some are very light and soft – this is the type used to make the heavenly dessert *coeur à la crème*. Others are richer and

Fromage Frais

spreadable, more like American CREAM CHEESE but sourer. French cream cheese is often flavoured with garlic, chives or black pepper.

MASCARPONE (MASCHERPONE)

ITALY

Mascarpone

This is hardly a cheese at all, but practically solid cream, with a fat content of 55–60%. It is made by heating and souring fresh cream, draining the resulting curd and then whipping it; the end result is thick and buttery, similar to English clotted cream but with a sour tang. In the past it was sold in small muslin bags, but today it is more likely to come in a carton. In Italy it is generally used like cream, or eaten as a dessert cheese, usually with fresh fruit, although in some districts it is mixed with anchovies, mustard and spices.

PETIT-SUISSE

FRANCE

This very mild, unsalted double-cream cheese is made from whole milk plus cream and sold in individual portions packed in cylindrical plastic cartons. It is eaten as it comes, or with sugar and fresh fruit. The name comes from its inventor, Mme Héroult, a Swiss lady living in Normandy in the 19th century. Her cheese was so successful that together with a partner, Charles Gervais, she started the Gervais cheese factory, now one of the largest in France.

PHILADELPHIA

UNITED STATES

Popularly known as 'Philly', this is the brand name of an American full-fat soft cheese first made in New York State in the late 19th century, and now widely exported. It is probably the top-selling packaged cheese in the world. The vogue for cheesecakes has increased sales of PHILADELPHIA because it is widely recommended for making them – it produces consistent results, being stabilized

Philadelphia

with carob gum. (Some recipes, not wishing to quote a brand name, specify 'processed cream cheese' – they mean Philly.) It comes in foil-wrapped packets and in tubs, and sometimes has added flavourings, such as chives or strawberry.

QUARK (QUARG)

GERMANY

This word simply means 'curd', and covers a whole family of curd cheeses which are

Quark (Quarg)

extremely popular in Germany – accounting for half their entire cheese consumption. It is very bland and smooth, and always low in fat. Skimmed-milk quark, MAGERQUARK, has less than 1%; low-fat quark, SPEISEQUARK, has 5% and medium-fat quark 10–12%. Exported quark is usually plain, but in Germany it can be flavoured with herbs, fruit purées or vegetables.

RAHMFRISCHKÄSE

GERMANY

Frischkäse is the German word for all types of fresh white cheese and *rahm* means cream, SO RAHMFRISCHKÄSE is simply a fresh CREAM CHEESE. It is made by adding cream to SPEISEQUARK to bring the fat content up to at least 50%. Double-cream cheese, DOPPELRAHMFRISCHKÄSE, has more cream and a fat content of at least 60%. They are easily spreadable, with a lightly sour, fresh taste. Export cheeses may be packed in small foil-sealed tubs, sometimes flavoured with horseradish and green herbs.

RONDELE

UNITED STATES

This is an American form of the French triple-cream cheese BOURSIN.

STRACCHINO CRESCENZA

ITALY

This fresh cheese from Lombardy is more solid than most, being ripened for 8–10 days. It can also be cut into slices, though only just. It is produced in rindless slabs, which have a soft and compact texture. The flavour is fresh and mild with a hint of acidity. Its fat content is 48–50%.

CHAPTER SEVEN

PLASTIC-CURD
AND
WHEY CHEESES

ost plastic-curd cheeses come from Italy, and the Italian name for them – *formaggio di pasta filata* (string cheese) – is a literal description of the way they are made. After preparing the curd the cheesemaker soaks it in hot whey until it becomes elastic. He then cuts it into small pieces and immerses it in hot water and whey. The dough-like paste is then kneaded until it can be pulled out into long threads or filaments. Finally the cheese is reshaped into large balls and immersed in the hot whey yet again. By this time it is so plastic it can be moulded into any shape that takes the cheesemaker's fancy.

Whey cheeses used to be the ultimate in economy, being made from the whey drained off after making other cheeses, which still contains nourishing milk protein and fats. Now they are often enriched with additional whole or skimmed milk. In Scandinavia such cheeses are made by gently heating whey until the water evaporates and the milk sugar turns into a brown, caramelized paste, which is why these cheeses have a rather sweet taste. Their fat content varies depending on the type and amount of milk added but is always low – around 20–30% in dry matter.

PLASTIC-CURD CHEESE

CACETTI

ITALY

These small, semi-hard pear-shaped cheeses are dipped in wax and suspended from a single long loop of raffia. They may also be wrapped in transparent plastic.

CACIOCAVALLO

ITALY

This is a very old cheese, known from at least as far back as Roman times. It is made

Kashkaval

throughout the eastern Mediterranean and Balkan regions under various similar names – KASHKAVAL in Bulgaria, KASHKAWAN in Syria and Lebanon, KASAR PEYNIR in Turkey and all mean 'cheese on horseback'. This is thought to refer to the fact that pairs of cheeses were strung together for ripening or smoking, and slung across a pole like saddle bags. The Italian version is made with cow's milk; others use sheep's, goat's or a mixture.

The shape of the cheese is unmistakable: a roundish oblong with a short neck and a ball on top, rather like an exaggerated pear, but bigger – an average one weighs around 4½ pounds (2 kg). The rind is smooth, thin, and pale yellow; the cheese slightly lighter, medium-hard and close-textured. When ripened for only three months, it has a mild delicate flavour and is eaten as a table cheese. Left for six months, it develops a stronger, fuller flavour and is used for cooking very much like PARMESAN.

KASSERI

GREECE

This Greek version of a plastic-curd cheese, made from sheep's or goat's milk, looks nothing like the Italian ones, as it is moulded into flat wheels or bars.

Although paler, almost white, it is similar in texture to PROVOLONE. The flavour is strong and salty. It is eaten as a table cheese, used to make pizzas, or dipped in flour and fried.

MANTECA (BURRINO)

ITALY

An ingenious invention, this consists of a pat of butter with cheese moulded round it to form a small ball or pear shape. This serves two purposes: it provides a portion of butter all ready to go with the cheese, and in pre-refrigeration days it kept the butter fresh. The names derive from the Spanish and Italian words for butter. The cheese itself may be MOZZARELLA, PROVOLONE or CACIOCAVALLO. The way to eat it is to slice the cheese open to reveal the butter; scoop it out, spread it on the bread and then add the cheese.

MOZZARELLA

ITALY

The word Mozzarella, familiar the world over as the cheese for making pizzas, can mean three quite different things. First comes the original MOZZARELLA DI BUFALA, made only from buffalo milk. This is the best, but hard to find and expensive. Next comes the milder Italian cow's milk MOZZARELLA, officially called FIOR DI LATTE – top of the milk. Finally there are the MOZZARELLAS made outside Italy – in the United States, Denmark, even Great Britain. The quality of these is extremely variable, and the worst brands are rubbery and totally tasteless. MOZZARELLA is different from other plastic-curd cheeses in being sold fresh – at

Mozzarella

best when only a few hours old. It should be soft and pure white, with a layered texture, an almost imperceptible shiny white rind, and a mild but slightly sour taste. The small balls of cheese are kept moist by either wrapping them up, tying the neck tightly, floating them in a bath of whey or sealing them into plastic.

The name Mozzarella is thought to date back to the early 15th century when the hand-spun cheese was cut or chopped – *mozzata*.

Italian MOZZARELLA is delicious eaten fresh with tomatoes, olives and anchovies. Domestic varieties are most often best kept for cooking. SCAMORZA is an expensive brined, sometimes smoked, form of MOZZARELLA.

PIZZA CHEESE

UNITED STATES

Sold especially for making pizzas, this is a domestic Mozzarella-like cheese with a lower moisture content which comes in large oblong blocks.

PROVOLONE

ITALY

Another well-known plastic-curd cheese, this is a familiar sight hanging from the ceilings of Italian delicatessens, inside its network of cords. The name means 'large oval' or 'sphere', but the cheese is produced in a variety of different shapes – pear,

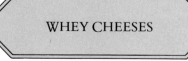

Provolone

cylinder, cone, sphere and melon. It is a medium-hard, smooth cow's-milk cheese, ivory-coloured, with a thin, shiny yellow rind.

PROVOLONE is another ancient cheese, and in Roman times it was eaten well matured, sometimes smoked. Today it is usually eaten when medium-ripe, after two to three months; in this form it is known as PROVOLONE DOLCE, and has a mild, delicate and creamy flavour. Small cheeses are sliced by removing wedges from in between the cords. PROVOLONE PICCANTE, aged for four to six months, is harder, darker and much stronger; it is suitable for grating.

Demand for PROVOLONE is so great that it is made in the United States and other countries, and sold under a multiplicity of brand names. The word is a registered trade name though and genuine PROVOLONE from Italy is labelled *Consorzio Formaggio Tipico Provolone*.

RAGUSANO

ITALY

This Provolone-type cheese from Ragusa in Sicily is moulded into loaf shapes. It can be eaten as a table cheese up to six months old, after which it is so hard it needs grating.

STRING CHEESE (BRAIDED CHEESE)

UNITED STATES

A special type of plastic-curd cheese brought over by immigrants from Armenia, which is formed into strips plaited or twisted into ropes. It tends to be rubbery and so tasteless that a flavouring of caraway or nigella seeds is often added.

WHEY CHEESES

GJETOST (GETOST)

NORWAY, SWEDEN

These words simply mean 'goat cheese' and

Gjetost (Getost)

refer to Scandinavian whey cheeses made with a mixture of goat's and cow's milk or goat's milk – EKTE GJETOST. They are basically the same as MYSOST (MESOST) but darker in colour.

MIZITHRA

GREECE

This cheese is made from the whey left behind after the making of FETA and KEFALOTIRI. But nowadays whole sheep's or cow's milk may be added to make it richer. It is a primitive cheese, made from ancient times and still presented in small baskets. Like RICOTTA it is eaten fresh, sometimes so fresh it is still warm.

In Cyprus, MIZITHRA is known as ANARI; in Turkey it is called NOOR.

MYSOST (MESOST)

NORWAY, SWEDEN

The cheese is extremely popular in these two countries and the names simply mean 'whey cheese'. It is a historic cheese which probably sustained the Vikings. In Norway today it accounts for 30% of all cheese produced. It is eaten for breakfast, put in sandwiches and used for cooking. The basic cheese is a medium-to dark-brown block with a rather sweet flavour. Milk, cream or buttermilk are added to make cheeses of various consistencies and fat content. Soft, spreadable varieties called MESSMÖR are sold in cartons.

RICOTTA

ITALY

The name of this cheese means cooked, referring to the fact that it is obtained by retreating the whey left after producing various other cheeses. Some are sheep's milk cheeses, like PECORINO ROMANO, others are cow's-milk cheese, which gives a blander flavour. Some RICOTTA is made from a mixture of the two. Nowadays whole or skimmed milk is added to make a richer cheese – American-made Ricotta contains up to 10% whole milk, and has a grainy texture due to vinegar being added as a preservative.

Ricotta

In its traditional form, it is a distinctive-looking cheese, moulded in the shape of an upturned basin with basketwork imprints on the surface. The most familiar cheese is *tipo dolce,* which is fresh, white and soft, with a delicately sour flavour (almost sweet when very fresh).

There is also a dry, salted version, ripened for a couple of months, known in Italy as *tipo moliterno.* This is firm enough to slice; similar to CREAM CHEESE or FARMER CHEESE.

Fresh RICOTTA is widely used in Italian cooking as a filling for pasta or a base for cheesecakes, and is often eaten as a dessert with fruit and sugar.

CHAPTER EIGHT

GOAT
AND
SHEEP CHEESES

In countries with pastures rich enough for cows, goat and sheep cheeses account for a very small percentage of the total cheese produced – but they may still be very popular. In other countries such as Greece, and in the Middle East, where conditions are mostly unsuitable for cows, sheep and goat cheeses account for virtually all the cheese produced.

All goat cheeses are chalk white with a distinctively tangy flavour which comes from the milk. They are usually eaten when fresh and very mild, but they may be aged and strong-tasting. Their texture ranges from very soft (often with an outer ring of creamy paste encircling a slightly drier centre), to firm and sliceable.

Sheep's milk cheeses are similar to but more variable than goat's milk cheeses. They include soft crumbly cheeses like FETA and the very hard, well-matured PECORINOS. The difference lies in the method of production. The former types of cheese are often very salty as the curds are lightly pressed, then soaked in brine solution. The latter are made like PARMESAN, being cooked and pressed. Some cheeses are made from either sheep's or goat's milk according to the time of year and availability.

Many goat cheeses come from France. If they are described as *chèvre* or *pur chèvre* they should by law contain only goat's milk. *Mi-chèvre* should have a minimum of 25% goat's mixed with cow's. *Lait de mélange* contains 10–15% goat's milk.

British-made goat and sheep cheeses were rare until quite recently, but small dairies are increasingly making them because if they use cow's milk they have to buy it centrally and pay the full retail price which makes their products hopelessly expensive.

Sheep's and goat's milks have higher food values than cow's milk. However the fat content of the cheeses described here is the usual 40–50% unless otherwise stated. With some of the more primitive cheeses fat content is likely to be variable.

BANON

FRANCE

A small round cheese from Provence, it is easily identified by its wrapping of chestnut leaves tied on with raffia. Farmhouse ones are made from goat's or sheep's milk, but factory versions will probably be cow's milk or *mi-chèvre* (mixed milk) cheeses. The delicious, mild flavour comes from soaking the leaves in brandy and slowly ripening the wrapped cheeses in earthenware jars.

Banon

POIVRE D'ANE is a similar cheese rolled in sprigs of savory and packed in savory-lined boxes.

BREBIS

FRANCE

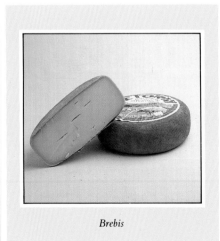

Brebis

The word means 'ewe' in French but it is also the term for a large mountain sheep's milk cheese from south-west France. Some are quite rare, but one, brand-named ETORKI, is more easily available. It is one of the few hard cheeses in this group, smooth-textured with an orange-brown washed rind and tangy flavour.

BRIN D'AMOUR

CORSICA

This semi-hard goat or sheep cheese is matured on beds of wild herbs which give it an exquisite flavour and aroma. It is made in blocks and the thin grey rind is covered with herbs, hence the name 'sprigs of love'.

BRYNDZA (BRYNZA, BRINZA)

EASTERN EUROPE

This cheese is made in the Carpathian Mountain regions of Poland, Czechoslovakia, Hungary and Romania, as well as in Bulgaria. The name simply means cheese. It is usually made from sheep's milk and is a white, brine-cured type with a resulting salty taste. Its texture ranges from soft and spreadable to firm and crumbly.

BUCHE DE CHEVRE (BUCHERON)

FRANCE

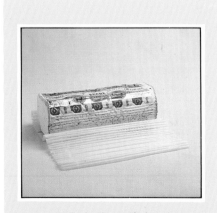

Bûche de Chèvre (Bûcheron)

The archetypal goat cheese, made in a log shape, with a soft white rind and slightly chalky inside. The flavour is mild but with a pleasant tang. Sometimes it is just called *bûche* – log.

CACHAT

FRANCE

One of the many purely local goat and sheep cheeses found in Provence, this one is usually made from sheep's milk. It is eaten fresh and has a very mild, almost sweet taste.

CAPRICORN

GREAT BRITAIN

This name is used for an English goat cheese made in Somerset. Similar names

Capricorn

(CAPRICORNE, CAPRICETTE, CAPRINO), are used in France and Italy for goat cheeses of various types.

CHABICHOU (CHABI)

FRANCE

A really 'goaty' goat cheese, with pronounced flavour and smell. It has been made for centuries in the province of Poitou, and comes in small truncated cones or cylinders. Farmhouse ones have light blue rinds speckled with red; factory ones, bloomy white rinds. The name is a dialect word for goat.

Chabichou (Chabi)

CHEVROTIN DES ARAVIS

FRANCE

This semi-hard, disk-shaped goat cheese made in Savoy, has a firm, greyish rind and is fairly mild in flavour. The name derives from the French for goat – any cheese with a name along these lines will be made wholly or partly from goat's milk.

CHEVROTIN PERSILLÉ DES ARAVIS is a great rarity: a blue-veined goat cheese. It has a rough natural rind and a sharp, rather salty taste.

CROTTIN DE CHAVIGNOL

FRANCE

A very small goat cheese made in flattened balls. When aged, these turn hard and brown, hence the unsavoury name – *crottin*

Crottin de Chavignol

means 'horse droppings'. At this stage the cheese is too pungent and salty to appeal to anyone not brought up on it, but it is usually eaten much younger and fresher, when it is enjoyably piquant. The French love it – they make millions of these cheeses each year and the name is protected.

FETA (FETTA)

GREECE, EASTERN EUROPE

Ancient Greek FETA was made with sheep's milk; modern Greek FETA may include some goat's or cow's milk. This can only be tasted in Greece, as it is so popular that demand exceeds supply and export is banned. The FETA sold on world markets is made in the United States, Denmark and various other countries from cow's milk although Bulgaria exports sheep's milk FETA.

The cheese is stark white and crumbly, with a sharp, salty taste due to it having been cured in brine. In Greece it is still floating in brine when bought, but

Danish Feta

elsewhere usually comes vacuum-packed. The name comes from the slabs or slices (*fetes*) into which it is cut. FETA is usually eaten after only about four weeks' ripening, when it is just firm enough to cut into cubes or crumble, and it has no rind. The cheese can also be left to mature for longer, when it becomes quite hard. The fat content varies between 45–60% depending on the type of milk used.

HALOUMI (HALLOUMI, HELLIM)

GREECE, CYPRUS

Like FETA this cheese is cured in brine, but it is rolled and kneaded to make it semi-hard and rubbery in texture. Its colour is ivory white, has a very salty taste, and is often rolled with mint leaves. It cooks well; in Cyprus it is often cubed or sliced and then fried or grilled. The cheese was originally made by nomadic Bedouin tribes, and is found all over the Middle East; the spelling of the names varies slightly. Native HALOUMI is always made from sheep's or cow's milk as far afield as Denmark and Australia.

KEFALOTIRI

GREECE

A hard cheese with dry natural rind, made in low cylinders, it is usually grated and used for cooking. The name means 'sheep's

Kefalotiri

head'. The milk used may be sheep's or goat's. The flavour is so strong that exported 'Kefalotiri' is likely to be another cheese called KEFALOGRAVIERA, which is a mixture of the strong cheese with a milder one, GRAVIERA.

MANCHEGO

SPAIN

A firm, pale-gold sheep's-milk cheese originally from the plain of La Mancha,

famous as the home of the fictional *Don Quixote*. It is made in low cylinders and has a natural rind which develops black mould as it ripens, but this is usually removed before the cheese is sold. It has a scattering of holes and its consistency varies as it comes in four grades: fresh *(fresca)*; cured for 3–13 weeks *(curado)*; aged for over 3 months *(viejo)*; or steeped in olive oil *(en aceite)*. The flavour is full and mellow, and the rich sheep's milk gives it a fat content of 50–60%. Not surprisingly it is Spain's most popular cheese and eaten in vast quantity.

NIOLO

CORSICA

This genuine rustic cheese is made exclusively on farms in the Corsican mountains. Usually made from sheep's milk but sometimes goat's, it can be eaten fresh, when it is quite mild, or ripened for three months, when it has a strong smell and flavour with a sharp aftertaste. After that it becomes very pungent indeed. NIOLO has a coarse, buttery texture and is roughly circular, being cured in baskets which leave their impression on the greyish-white rind. Sometimes it is wrapped in dried herbs.

PECORINO ROMANO

ITALY

Pecorino is the Italian name for any sheep's-milk cheese, but this is one of the oldest, recorded by the Roman writer Pliny, and its name is protected. It is a cheese similar to PARMESAN – grainy-textured and hard, mainly used for grating, though it can be eaten as a table cheese when fairly young (the minimum ageing period is eight months). It has a higher fat content (36%) and a strong aroma which some find unpleasant but leads others to prefer it to PARMESAN. It is pale, almost white and made in large cylinders with a white-waxed rind stamped with a sheep's head.

PECORINO SICILIANO and PECORINO SARDO are similar cheeses made in Sicily

and Sardinia. FIORE SARDO ('flower of Sardinia') is softer, with a darker rind, and is used as a table cheese up to six months old, and used grated after that.

PYRAMIDES

FRANCE

As some goat cheeses are known simply as logs after their shape, so others are called pyramids, since they are shaped into a flat-topped pyramid. They are mostly small,

Valencay

with white rinds, and may be matured in edible charcoal *(cendré)* which gives them a dusty, blue-black surface and strong charcoal smell. The flavour ranges from mild to sharp according to age.

LEZAY is a well-known pyramid, which also comes in log form. VALENCAY is another, with superb flavour, especially if farmhouse made. POULIGNY-SAINT-PIERRE and SELLES-SUR-CHER are ones with protected names. The first sometimes comes wrapped in leaves.

RIGOTTE

FRANCE

A very small cylindrical cheese with a thin, orange rind and salty flavour. Usually packed in jars with olive oil and herbs, it was originally a pure goat cheese, but may now be *mi-chèvre* or even all cow. The name is thought originally to have been *recuite,*

Rigotte

SAINT-MARCELLIN

FRANCE

Le Pitchou

meaning that, like RICOTTA, it was originally a recooked or whey cheese.

Farmhouse versions of this cheese used to be made of goat's milk, but they are fast disappearing and factory ones are all or part cow's milk. It comes in small, almost single-portion disks, with thin bloomy rind just tinged with greeny-blue mould. The texture is soft and flavour milk.

A version packed in jars with olive oil and herbs is known as LE PITCHOU.

SAINT-MAURE

FRANCE

A classic goat cheese with a protected name, made in small logs which, if farmhouse-made, have a straw run through the middle to hold the soft, creamy cheese together. Its flavour is strong. The rind has a white mould, tinged pinky brown.

CHAPTER NINE

FLAVOURED CHEESES

Most traditional cheeses owe their flavour to the type of milk from which they are made, plus added salt. This intensifies during the ripening period; a long-matured cheese has more flavour than a young one. Mould growth is another way of introducing additional flavour. Special treatments such as coating the cheese with ash or charcoal or wrapping it in leaves or herbs can also affect its taste.

The cheeses in this chapter are ones where the natural flavour has been enhanced or complemented by adding extra ingredients such as herbs, spices, wine or nuts. These are added to the basic cheese, which is sometimes coated with the flavouring as well.

Although the practice of flavouring cheese has a long history, it has become increasingly popular in recent years, paradoxically running alongside the modern taste for milder cheeses.

Flavoured cheeses are extremely popular in the United States, and almost any type of plain cheese can be had in a flavoured form. Flavourings used range from cumin, jalapeño chilli peppers and sage to meats, vegetables and fruit.

In addition to the named cheeses listed here, many soft fresh cheeses are available with added flavourings.

APPLEWOOD (CHARNWOOD)

GREAT BRITAIN

Applewood (Charnwood)

A smoke-flavoured CHEDDAR covered with paprika.

BOULETTE D'AVESNES

FRANCE

An unusual-looking small cheese, like a plump, dark-orange cone. Parsley, tarragon and pepper are kneaded into the

Boulette d'Avesnes

cone-shaped cheese which is then washed with beer during the ripening period. The result is a cheese with a marzipan-like texture, a potent spicy flavour and a strong smell.

CHEVIOT

GREAT BRITAIN

This is a delicately flavoured Cheddar cheese incorporating chopped chives.

CHEVRETTE

FRANCE

Logs of fresh, nearly triple-cream, goat's-milk cheese, flavoured with garlic and a variety of herbs. The fat content is high at 70%.

COTSWOLD

GREAT BRITAIN

DOUBLE GLOUCESTER flavoured with chives and onions.

Cotswold

GAPERON (GAPRON)

FRANCE

A country-style cheese strongly flavoured with garlic or peppercorns. Made from skimmed milk or buttermilk, it has a low fat content (35%). The shape, like an upturned pudding basin tied up in yellow

Gaperon (Gapron)

raffia, is very distinctive. The rind is bloomy white, the cheese inside ivory-coloured and very soft, particularly in the centre.

FRIESIAN CHEESE (FRIESE NAGELKAAS)

HOLLAND

Clove-and cumin-flavoured cheese which comes from the Friesland district of Holland, home of the now world-famous

Friesan Cheese

Huntsman

Leiden

black and white cows. It is also known as 'nail cheese', a reference to the nail-like shape of a whole clove. Made in wheels and aged for at least six months, the cheese is greyish-white, hard and dry, with a tough rind. Its fat content varies from as little as 20% to a moderate 40%.

GEROME ANISE

FRANCE

A version of the soft ripened cheese MUNSTER GÉRÔMÉ flavoured with cumin seeds for a mildly spicy taste.

HOPFENKÄSE (NIEHEIMER HOPFENKÄSE)

GERMANY

Small and round, these acid-curd cheeses are flavoured with caraway seeds and ripened in between layers of hops *(Hopfen)*. This gives them a pronounced spicy, hoppy flavour. Farmhouse versions can be hard enough for grating; factory ones are semi-soft.

HUNTSMAN

GREAT BRITAIN

In this cheese layers of STILTON are alternated with layers of DOUBLE GLOUCESTER. Sometimes called the 'E' cheese because of its distinctive appearance when cut.

ILCHESTER

GREAT BRITAIN

Ilchester

DOUBLE GLOUCESTER flavoured with mustard pickle.

JALAPEÑO JACK

UNITED STATES

MONTEREY JACK cheese flavoured with jalapeño chilli peppers.

LEIDEN

HOLLAND

A harder, drier cheese than the familiar EDAM and GOUDA, LEIDEN has a piquant flavour due to a liberal content of cumin seeds. A whole cheese is wheel-shaped; factory ones have natural dry rinds but farmhouse ones have red-dyed rinds

stamped with crossed keys, the coat of arms of the city of Leiden. Farmhouse LEIDEN is a medium-fat cheese (30%); factory ones usually have 40% fat but sometimes only 20%.

LIPTAUER (LIPTAUER BRYNDZA)

HUNGARY, CZECHOSLOVAKIA

Originally this was a fresh sheep's-milk cheese, credited to Liptó, an area in the Tatra mountains. In the rest of Europe and the United States the name has come to mean any fresh white or pot cheese flavoured and tinted pink with paprika. Sometimes other ingredients such as chopped onion, caraway seeds and mustard are added. In Austria a version is made called LIPTAUER GARNIERT.

NØKKELOST (KUMINOST)

NORWAY

A version of the Dutch LEIDEN, this is a semi-hard cheese flavoured with cumin seeds. *Nøkkel* means keys and recalls the crossed-keys symbol, the coat of arms of Leiden.

NUTWOOD

GREAT BRITAIN

CHEDDAR flavoured with hazelnuts, raisins and cider.

PEPPER BRIE

FRANCE, GERMANY

The ever-popular BRIE is now available with added flavourings; crushed black peppercorns are the most popular.

Pepper Brie

Sometimes they are just sprinkled on the rind, sometimes distributed through the cheese as well. Other flavourings include herbs, paprika and mushrooms.

POIVRE D'AUVERGNE

FRANCE

A recently introduced semi-hard cheese with a distinctive shiny black artificial rind, it is very smooth and bland, and heavily flavoured with crushed black peppercorns.

PORT WINE CHEDDAR

UNITED STATES

Port Wine Cheddar

A popular COLDPACK CHEESE flavoured with domestic port wine.

QUATRIN

FRANCE

A recently introduced cheese lightly flavoured with garlic and parsley. It has a highly distinctive appearance, resembling a

Quatrin

9-inch (23 cm) round cake moulded into four petals, and is pure white with green packaging. It is a young soft-ripened cheese, sold after 2 weeks' maturing. Its fat content is 60%.

LE ROULE

FRANCE

This is a popular range of fresh, full fat soft cheeses which are rolled up round the

Le Roulé

flavouring like a Swiss (jelly) roll. The flavouring – herb, spice or strawberry – is also coated on the outside of the roll.

RUTLAND

GREAT BRITAIN

Rutland

CHEDDAR flavoured with beer, garlic and parsley.

SAGE CHEESES

GREAT BRITAIN

SAGE DERBY, marbled green with sage leaf juice, is more popular than the original DERBY. But SAGE LANCASHIRE, flavoured with actual chopped sage leaves, is even harder to find than good LANCASHIRE.

SAPSAGO (SCHABZIEGER)

SWITZERLAND

A strange cheese, greeny-grey in colour, and shaped into a small hard cone. It has a strong flavour, which comes from a special variety of clover-blue melitot. It is most often grated and sprinkled on food. The fat content is negligible (3%) as it is made from skimmed milk. It is an ancient, primitive cheese; the name is a corruption of the original Swiss place name. It is also known as green cheese or GLARNERKÄSE.

SHERWOOD

GREAT BRITAIN

DOUBLE GLOUCESTER with sweet pickle.

SMOKED CHEESES

AUSTRIA, GERMANY

Usually sausage-shaped, with a reddish-brown, glossy rind, these cheeses have a smooth texture and bland flavour with a pleasant, smoky tang. They are often processed but not always. SMOKED CHEESES can also come enriched with chopped ham. The fat content ranges from 45–60%. Austrian and German SMOKED CHEESES really are smoked, not just given a synthetic smoky flavour, as is often the case with cheeses made outside these countries. They are commonly found ready cut and packaged in thick slices.

VERMONT SAGE

UNITED STATES

Sage-flavoured version of a superior American cheese, VERMONT CHEDDAR.

WALTON

GREAT BRITAIN

A mixture of CHEDDAR and STILTON flavoured and coated with chopped walnuts.

WINDSOR RED

GREAT BRITAIN

CHEDDAR marbled with elderberry wine.

Windsor Red

CHAPTER TEN

PROCESSED CHEESES

Although most processed cheeses are invariably bland and do not appeal to connoisseurs, they are an important part of the world cheese scene and play a big role in the national diet of many nations. Something like one third of all cheese produced in the United States ends up being processed. In Japan, it is by far the most popular cheese, and processed GRUYÈRE is an important Swiss export.

Processed cheese was developed by the Swiss in the first decade of the 19th century to overcome the marketing problems associated with natural cheeses, particularly in the absence of refrigeration. Cheese has a tendency to spoil rapidly, becoming overripe and unpalatable, if not kept in the right conditions. Large Swiss cheeses like EMMENTAL and GRUYÈRE were also very difficult to handle in the relatively primitive shipping and storage facilities of the time. Processing also provided a way of using cheeses which were perfectly edible but not up to standard.

Processing natural cheeses solved all these problems, producing a range of cheese products which were sterile – so kept almost indefinitely – and which could be packaged in whatever form was convenient to the manufacturer, distributor and seller. Today the most familiar packaging is the shallow round box containing foil-wrapped triangles of cheese. Processed cheese is infinitely malleable though, as the myriad of different forms and brands on sale testify. It can be packed in just about any conceivable sort of container – practical or decorative. It can be soft enough to pack in a tube or tub, or hard enough to pre-cut into convenient sandwich-shaped slices or mould into a block.

HOW PROCESSED CHEESE IS MADE

The basic ingredient is a natural cheese, often EMMENTAL, GRUYÈRE or CHEDDAR. Sometimes a mixture of two or three cheeses is used. After removal of the rind or any artificial coating, the cheese is cut up and very finely ground. Emulsifying salts are then added, together with any further ingredients – more fat, whey powder, water, and often flavourings such as herbs, spices, nuts or pieces of cured meat. The resulting paste-like mass is heated under carefully controlled conditions which change the character of the cheese in several stages. The end result is a liquid cheese product with a smooth glossy texture, retaining as much of the flavour of the original cheese as possible. While still warm and semi-liquid this is fed into an automatic filling and wrapping machine to emerge ready for sale in the required shape and weight.

The United States Department of Agriculture recognizes three distinct types of product: Processed Cheese of a particular type, such as processed CHEDDAR; Processed Cheese and Cheese Spread; and Process Cheese Products or Foods, the ones that contain additional flavourings. The fat and moisture content of all these cheeses is strictly regulated by law. Many other countries also have specific standards. All types of processed cheese are soft to semi-soft, nearly always rindless, with an elastic texture and mild flavour.

The words *Crème de . . .* or *Crema di* on the label of French and Italian cheeses respectively indicate that they are processed.

WHY CHOOSE PROCESSED CHEESE?

In the early days the use of inferior cheeses for processing gave some types a bad name, but today the legal requirements mentioned above ensure that a uniform high quality is one of the hallmarks of processed cheese. This is one of the reasons some people prefer it. It can be relied on to be nice to eat; it may never rival the sublime taste of a perfectly ripened BRIE, but neither will it offend like one that has become overripe.

Because processed cheese is a product, and not a natural food, it comes in great variety; every country has its own established types and favourites. Run-of-the-mill processed cheeses are made with a mixture of whatever cheese is cheap and in surplus, which is often enriched with vegetable fat. Fine processed cheeses, some of which come from France (the home of so many great natural cheeses) are made either from a single named cheese, usually GRUYÈRE, or from a fixed recipe of named cheeses, and are enriched with butter or cream. They must have a minimum fat content of 40% and maximum moisture content of 50%.

Here are a few well-known processed cheeses.

PROCESSED CHEDDAR

GREAT BRITAIN, UNITED STATES

There is not much to be said about this except that it is made in blocks and is always the cheapest cheese in the supermarket.

A great deal of AMERICAN CHEDDAR is sold in processed form, either as blocks, or in the form of packaged processed products or spreads in an incredibly wide range of shapes, sizes and flavouring. VELVEETA and KRAFT are among the well-known and exported brands.

CHEESE SPREADS

INTERNATIONAL

Primula

This type of processed cheese has a higher moisture content, so that it spreads readily. It is available in enormous variety; the base cheeses used depend on the country of origin. One of the oldest, now sold world-wide, is PRIMULA, developed by a Norwegian, Olav Kavli, in 1924. Cheese spreads can be flavoured with ham, shrimp, lobster, crab, mixed vegetables, celery, chives, mixed herbs, pepper, pineapple – you name it, somebody makes it. Nowadays the cheeses are often conveniently packed in tubes so that you can quickly squeeze out exactly what you want, leaving the rest in perfect condition.

In France, cheese spread is called *fromage pour tartines* (cheese for sandwiches), which implies a moisture content above 50%.

FONDU

FRANCE

Fromage fondu is the French word for any type of processed cheese. Everyday ones are made in triangles like the Swiss LA VACHE QUI RIT (the Laughing Cow) brand.

Fondu aux Raisins

Fine French processed cheeses are made to look like natural ones.

FONDU AUX RAISINS or Grape Cheese is a popular processed version of TOMME AUX RAISINS, made in drums with a thick coating of black wax encrusted with dried grape pips. Unlike the rind on the original cheese this is not edible.

Rambol

FONDU AUX POIVRES and FONDU AU KIRSCH are similar but rindless cheeses flavoured with peppercorns and kirsch.

FONDU AUX NOIX is a large flat cake-like cheese (also known as GÂTEAU AUX NOIX) covered with walnuts, with another layer of walnuts running through the centre. Processed cheese containing various added flavourings is also sold under the brand names REYBIER and RAMBOL.

PROCESSED GRUYERE

SWITZERLAND

This is the original processed cheese invented in Switzerland, also known as PETIT GRUYÈRE and SWISS TRIANGLES. The

Processed Gruyère (Tiger)

traditional packaging is the round box containing 6 or 12 foil-wrapped triangles, but it now also comes as 6 or 12 sandwich-shaped slices, or in foil bags ready for making instant fondu.

The principle brands of PETIT GRUYÈRE are CHALET, FROMALP, MILKBOY, SWISS CASTLE, SWISS KNIGHT, TIGER and ZINGG. Sometimes these are flavoured with herbs or wine, or have other cheeses added.

HI-MELT CHEESES

UNITED STATES

Processed cheese does not cook well as it tends to lose its flavour easily. Hi-melt cheeses were developed to overcome this problem. There are two types, both CHEDDAR-based: Hi-melt processed cheese and Hi-melt processed cheese food. The former contains more fat and less moisture and has a stronger flavour.

SCHMELZKÄSE

GERMANY

Schmelzkäse

This is the German term for processed cheese. Such cheeses are widely exported, one of the most popular being the smoked type made in the form of a large sausage, with or without chopped ham flavouring. They are genuinely smoked, not just endowed with a synthetic smoke flavour.

CHAPTER ELEVEN

VEGETARIAN
AND
SLIMMERS' CHEESES

heese is an important source of protein, but it presents difficulties for three distinct groups: vegetarians, those observing Jewish or other dietary laws, and health-conscious people who want to cut their fat intake, either to lose weight or reduce cholesterol levels.

Cheese of any kind is out for the strictest kind of vegetarians, or vegans, who do not eat any animal products. There are, nonetheless, many other vegetarians who would eat cheese, if it did not contain animal rennet. The Jewish dietary laws prohibit the mixing of milk and milk products with meat, so animal rennet is once again a problem. Some cheeses, notably the Portuguese QUEIJO DE SERRA, were traditionally made with vegetable rennet produced from the flowers and leaves of a wild thistle and other plants, but today some producers of this type of cheese may use a little animal rennet as well, and unless it states this on the label or wrapper, there is no way this can be detected in the cheese. So the only real answer is a factory-made cheese guaranteed to be vegetarian or kosher. Fortunately these are to be found, even if not in every supermarket. Israel is a large producer of kosher versions of European cheeses, which are widely exported. In Great Britain, various small dairies are producing cheeses made with non-animal rennet in response to demand from an increasing number of vegetarians. Kosher cheeses are also produced in the United States, Holland and Switzerland.

For the health-conscious, the problem is not the animal rennet but the high fat and calorie content of some cheeses. Here again the dairy industry has come to the rescue, this time with a large number of low-fat cheeses. Unfortunately these are often not the most delicious or tasty cheeses; so this section of the book also points the way to selecting the most low-fat of the traditional cheeses.

If you happen to be on a vegetarian or kosher diet and also wish to lose weight or cut cholesterol there is even a cheese for you – some vegetarian CHEDDAR is made from skimmed milk, so the fat content is considerably reduced.

FAT AND CALORIE CONTENTS

Assessing how fattening a particular cheese is can be a complicated process. The calories come mainly from the fat content: as this is usually expressed as a percentage of the dry matter, it can look as if BRIE and CHEDDAR, for example, with very similar ratings (45%, 48%), have about the same number of calories. They don't, because a piece of BRIE contains more moisture than a piece of CHEDDAR of the same weight. What a slimmer needs to know is the fat content of the whole cheese. As this is rarely given it's safer to go by calorie counts. See the end of this chapter for a table of calorie counts of 50 popular cheeses.

Slimmers need to stick exclusively to the really low-fat, low-calorie cheeses. However, for all-round sensible eating there's no reason to deny yourself the wonderful flavours of natural cheese. Just pick the relatively low-calorie cheeses. Also, try eating cheese *instead of* rather than after meat, and restrict portions to 2 oz (60 g) for each adult.

ISRAELI KOSHER CHEESES

Bashan

Galil

The following are some brand names of guaranteed kosher cheeses. All are made from pasteurized milk, which may be cow's, sheep's or goat's, coagulated with non-animal rennet.

ATZMON – Bel Paese/Saint-Paulin type.

BASHAN – smoked, sausage-shaped cheese.

EIN-GEDI – Camembert type, foil wrapped.

GAD – something like Danbo – the name comes from *G'vina Denit* – Danish cheese.

GALIL – blue-veined sheep's-milk cheese modelled on Roquefort.

GILBOA – Edam type.

GILEAD – *pasta filata* type.

GOLAN – hard *pasta filata* type like Provolone.

JIZRAEL, TAL HA'EMEK – hard cheeses with holes like Emmental.

KOL-BEE – loaf-shaped Gouda type.

BRITISH VEGETARIAN CHEESES

BOTTON

This cheese is not only made with non-animal rennet, but with unpasteurized cow's milk; so it has a very fine flavour. It is semi-hard, comes from Danby in Yorkshire and is made according to a traditional recipe. It may not be easy to find outside its home ground.

CHEDDAR

Various vegetarian Cheddar-type cheeses are fairly widely available, sometimes in supermarkets, more often in health or natural food stores and specialist cheese shops. Naturally they are not all the same, but tend to be very similar to a young, mild CHEDDAR, and good for both eating and cooking.

DEVON GARLAND

Another delicious-sounding cheese, made from the rich unpasteurized milk of Jersey cows. It is semi-hard, but moist and crumbly like Caerphilly, with a layer of

Devon Garland

fresh herbs sandwiched in the centre. Named for a Devonshire village, it is made near Barnstaple.

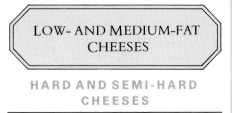

LOW- AND MEDIUM-FAT CHEESES

HARD AND SEMI-HARD CHEESES

In Great Britain, several branded cheeses are available which have half the fat content of the originals. Well-established ones are TENDALE CHESHIRE or CHEDDAR; and SHAPE CHEDDAR. These average 75 calories per oz (30 g).

Two fairly hard Dutch cheeses, LEIDEN and FRIESIAN CHEESE, are made in low-fat

forms (20% fat in dry matter). SAPSAGO (SCHABZIEGER) is made from skimmed milk and is extremely low in fat (3%) but high in protein, earning it the name, 'poor man's cheese'. All of these may be hard to find.

All types of German HANDKÄSE or HAND CHEESE are low in fat (below 10% in dry matter).

Most other hard cheeses are fairly high-fat because they contain less moisture than soft ones. As the French are very fond of pointing out, BRIE and CAMEMBERT have fewer calories, weight for weight, than CHEDDAR or GOUDA. On this principle the most villainous cheese of all should be PARMESAN, with even lower moisture content, but fortunately it is made from partially skimmed milk which brings the fat/calorie count down.

SOFT RIPENED CHEESES

Because of their higher moisture content, this group tends to be lower in calories than most hard cheeses. But watch out: the figures given here, and quoted in standard calorie tables, are for traditional cheeses with fat in dry matter contents of 40–45%. Quite a few of the newer soft ripened cheeses around are double or triple creams with fat contents of 60% and 75%. Where these are listed in this book, any exceptional fat content is always mentioned. If you cannot be sure of the fat content of an unfamiliar soft ripened cheese, a rich creamy taste is a pretty reliable indicator that it's high-fat. A very soft texture may not be – VIGNOTTE is a much firmer cheese than double-cream CAMEMBERT or BRIE, but clocks up a horrifying 72%.

The washed-rind cheeses LIMBURGER and ROMADUR are both made in low-fat (20%) forms and are excellent if you can find them.

BLUE-VEINED CHEESES

In Britain the TENDALE range of cheeses now includes a reduced-fat blue cheese which rates 145 calories per 2-oz (50-g)

portion – 115 less than the same portion of Stilton.

The table at the end of the book includes calorie counts for some of the most popular blue cheeses. The main thing to keep off is BLUE BRIE of any kind, as its fat content is at least 50% and sometimes 70% in dry matter.

FRESH CHEESES

This group can easily lead would-be slimmers astray, as it contains everything from no-fat and low-fat to wicked triple-creams. See the Fresh Cheese chapter for details of individual cheeses.

The no-fat cheese is FROMAGE BLANC. This can be used as a substitute in most dishes that call for cream.

COTTAGE CHEESE is made for slimmers. It is easy to recognize by its carton packaging and granular texture, and the fat content is only 4%. Added flavourings make it more tasty without greatly increasing calorie counts (but beware ones containing mayonnaise, and, in the United States, whipped cream). Some manufacturers now make half-fat COTTAGE CHEESE, which usually contains added flavourings to zip it up a bit.

With soft fresh cheeses, look for packets labelled 'low-fat', or at least 'full-fat'; avoid those labelled double- or triple-cream.

German QUARK comes in three grades; SPEISEQUARK, the middle one with 5% fat, equates with COTTAGE CHEESE.

OTHER CHEESES

PLASTIC-CURD AND WHEY CHEESES

Hard plastic-curd cheeses like PROVOLONE have standard 40–45% fat content; MOZZARELLA and PIZZA CHEESE, with much higher moisture contents, are the ones to pick. Whey cheeses are inherently low-fat and again RICOTTA, with high moisture content, is the best of all. But check before buying – nowadays varying amounts of milk are added to the whey, so two identical-looking RICOTTAS may vary considerably in calorie content.

GOAT AND SHEEP CHEESES

Some goat cheeses are surprisingly low-calorie, but not all, and you can't tell the difference by their appearance. BANON, CHÈVRE logs, SAINT-MAURE and SAINT-

MARCELLIN are all good choices. FETA and HALOUMI are equally good.

FLAVOURED CHEESES

The English cheeses in this group have the same average fat rating as their plain originals, and so are not much good to the would-be slimmer. GAPERON is a goat cheese and one of the low-calorie ones. Avoid the new cream-enriched cheeses such as some flavoured BRIES and

QUATRIN. See also the hard flavoured cheeses mentioned above, LEIDEN, FRIESIAN CHEESE and SAPSAGO.

PROCESSED CHEESE AND CHEESE SPREADS

Standard types usually have a minimum fat content of around 40%, although several low-fat types have been introduced during the 1980s.

CALORIE COUNT FOR 50 CHEESES

	CALORIES PER 1 OZ/30 G		CALORIES PER 1 OZ/30 G
Bel Paese	94–98	Limburger	73
Bleu d'Auvergne	97	Lymeswold	120
Bleu de Bresse	80	Melbury	91
Blue Brie	120–125	Mozzarella (Danish, Italian)	98, 97
Boursin	116	Munster	92
Brie	88	Mycella	99
Caerphilly	120	Parmesan	118
Camembert	88–95	Pecorino Romano, Pecorino Sardo	126
Cheddar, factory and farmhouse	120, 145	Philadelphia	90
Cheshire	110	Port-Salut	94–98
Chèvre log (goat cheese)	84	Processed cheese with walnuts	110 (average)
Double Gloucester	105	Provolone	98
Emmental	115	Pyramids (goat cheese)	98
Edam	90	Pyrénés cheese (cow)	102
Feta	85	Ricotta	55–58
Fondu aux Raisins	97	Roquefort	88
Fontal/Fontina	109	Saint-Paulin	94–98
Gorgonzola/Dolcelatte	112, 100	Sbrinz	124
Gouda	100	Shropshire Blue	116
Gruyère	117	Stilton (blue, white)	131, 108
Havarti	121	Taleggio	101
Jarlsberg	100	Tilsiter	117
Lancashire	109	Tomme aux Raisins	94
Leicester	105	Triple-cream cheese	103
Leiden	101	Wensleydale	115

TRAVELLERS' CHEESES

he cheeses listed here are only a brief sample of unfamiliar ones likely to be encountered on foreign holidays or business trips. They include a country's best-known popular cheese, the equivalent of British and American CHEDDAR; some known to be particularly delicious; and a few of special interest. These cheeses are of course in addition to the exported ones listed in the main sections of this book, and do not include local imitations of world-renowned cheeses. Most are cow's-milk cheeses with a fat content of 40–50%, but there are some very primitive ones whose fat content is too variable to pin down.

The bulk of cheeses from some countries are mainly goat's- or sheep's-milk cheeses or are eaten fresh: in which case these may be found in the appropriate main sections. Those cheeses which are purely local will be found in this section.

The best place to find local cheeses, apart from world-famous food stores like Androuet in Paris and Dallmay's in Münich, is in small shops and on market stalls; also in bars and restaurants where local people go. The list of translations of the word 'cheese' at the back of the book may be helpful.

NORTH AND SOUTH AMERICA

OKA

CANADA

A semi-soft cheese created at a Trappist monastery in Oka, Quebec in the late 19th century and modelled on PORT-SALUT, it is now factory-made.

RICHELIEU

CANADA

A copy of BEL PAESE which developed a character all of its own. It is brick-shaped,

with a lightly-washed reddish rind; texture and taste resemble factory-made BRIE.

QUESO FRESCO, QUESO BLANCO

LATIN AMERICA

Generic terms for fresh white cheese, widely-made and given different names in different countries.

ANEJO

MEXICO

The local soft, fresh, white cheese, made from skimmed goat's milk. Its shape and fat content vary, although it is often like a dry FETA.

ENCHILADO is the same cheese thickly covered in chilli powder and is not surprisingly fiendishly hot.

ASADERO (OAXACA)

MEXICO

Hard plastic-curd cheese similar to PROVOLONE, packed in plastic bags. Sometimes called OAXACA after the region where it was originally made. The best ASADERO comes from the state of Coahuila where the milk is rich in butterfat. Fat content below 30%.

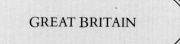

GREAT BRITAIN

CAMBRIDGE AND COLWICK

ENGLAND

Two traditional, soft, fresh, unsalted cheeses now enjoying a revival. CAMBRIDGE is made in rectangles on a straw base and has a creamy layer in the middle. COLWICK is very similar but comes in a flat round with upturned edges.

MOLLINGTON

ENGLAND

Hard smoked cheese from Oxfordshire.

BLARNEY

IRELAND

A semi-hard cheese with red rind, lots of holes and a mild flavour. Sometimes called 'Irish Swiss', but it is closer to Danish SAMSOE.

CROWDIE

SCOTLAND

This fresh cheese is farm-made from unpasteurized skimmed milk enriched with cream. Very rich and buttery – known locally as 'cruddy' (curdy) butter – it has a pleasantly sour taste.

DUNLOP

SCOTLAND

A moist, bland version of CHEDDAR. Usually eaten very young, it comes from Dunlop in Ayrshire. FARMHOUSE DUNLOP is the best, but rarely found.

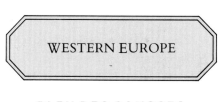

WESTERN EUROPE

BLEU DES CAUSSES

FRANCE

This is a blue-veined cheese on the lines of BLEU D'AUVERGNE but saltier. From Les Causses, limestone country which provides the caves required for ripening. The name is protected.

BLEU DE GEX, BLEU DE SEPTMONCEL

FRANCE

Both these are very fine blue-veined cheeses from the Jura mountains entitled to the protected name BLEU DU HAUT-JURA.

CANTAL

FRANCE

The French 'Cheddar', one of their oldest cheeses, it has been made in and around

Cantal

Cantal in the mountains of the Auvergne for over 2,000 years. Also known as FOURME DE CANTAL and SALERS; all three are protected names.

CHESTER

FRANCE

Gallic version of an English-style cheese, something like a cross between CHEDDAR and CHESHIRE.

CURE NANTAIS (FROMAGE DU CURE)

FRANCE

A major cheese in Britanny and named after the 19th-century priest who invented it. It is a typical washed-rind cheese, with pungent flavour and smell, made in small rectangles.

MAMIROLLE

FRANCE

Recently invented, this is a brick-shaped cheese, tasting and smelling like a tamed LIMBURGER.

MIMOLETTE

FRANCE

A large ball-shaped cheese like a double-size EDAM, but dyed orange and lacking the red rind. Some is made in France, but much is imported COMMISSIEKAAS from Holland and rechristened for the French market.

Mimolette

MORBIER

FRANCE

When cut open this cheese reveals a horizontal line of black ash dividing the smooth, pale-yellow body. This is edible, recalling the days when it was made from two batches of curd and soot was smeared over the first to protect it. Made in large wheels with a dry natural rind, it has a mild flavour.

POLDER

HOLLAND

This is a brand name cheese with a black, waxed rind contrasting strongly with the orange-yellow interior. Smooth and buttery with a tangy aftertaste, Polder is made in big drums.

ROLLOT

FRANCE

Another cheese for the brave: rich and creamy, but with an orange-red washed rind giving it a powerful smell and taste similar to MAROILLES. It is made in small rounds or heart shapes.

BIANCO

GERMANY

The brand name of an almost white, rather rich (55% fat) block-shaped cheese full of small holes. Rather like TILSIT.

RAHM BRIE (RAHM CAMEMBERT)

GERMANY

German-made versions of these two classic cheeses using milk with a higher fat content.

WEINKÄSE

GERMANY

Very small 2½-oz (75-g), mild, semi-soft cheese, just right for enjoying with a glass of wine. Made in thick rounds and sold under many brand names, they are often packed in pairs.

WEISSLACKERKÄSE (BIERKÄSE)

GERMANY

Semi-soft cheese with waxy white ('white-lacquered') rind, made in 2-oz (60-g) cubes. Its flavour resembles smoked bacon, and is strong to pungent, depending on age – when fully matured it resembles LIMBURGER. It is also known as BIERKÄSE (BEER CHEESE).

GRAVIERA

GREECE

Strictly speaking this is a copycat cheese – a version of GRUYÈRE. But it is the second most popular Greek cheese after FETA. It is made from cow's milk, whereas virtually all other Greek cheeses are made with sheep's milk.

KERNHEM

HOLLAND

This double-cream (60% fat) monastery-style cheese with an orange, washed rind is made in small flat rounds. It tastes like a strong SAINT-PAULIN.

WHITE MAY CHEESE

HOLLAND

A fresh version of GOUDA, eaten when only 2–3 days old. White in colour with a slightly sour taste.

White May Cheese

CACIOTTA

ITALY

Literally 'little cheese', this word describes a multiplicity of small, semi-soft, locally made cheeses which vary in form and flavour from place to place.

ITALICO

ITALY

Generic term for a family of semi-soft mild cheeses similar to BEL PAESE.

ROBIOLA

ITALY

A hard-to-track-down cheese – it can be round, square or rectangular, and made from any kind of milk. However, it should always feature the reddish rind for which it is named (from the Latin *rubium*). It is a soft, washed-rind cheese, somewhat similar to TALEGGIO, delicate and mild when young.

CABRALES

SPAIN

Blue-veined cheese from the mountains of Asturias in northern Spain, generally made with cow's milk, although sometimes mixed milk is used. It may be wrapped in blackened sycamore leaves.

CEBRERO

SPAIN

A strange-looking cheese like a thick-stalked mushroom with overlapping cap. Made from cow's milk, it is semi-hard with a medium-strong flavour.

MAHON

SPAIN

This one is square and semi-soft, with a pale creamy, small-holed interior, patchy yellowish-brown natural rind and mellow flavour. It is made from cow's milk, sometimes mixed with sheep's, on the Balearic Islands, particularly Minorca.

ALPKÄSE

SWITZERLAND

'Cheese from the Alps' describes many kinds of locally made typically Swiss cheeses made in wheels with lots of holes.

EASTERN EUROPE

PODHALANSKI

POLAND

Brick-shaped, semi-hard cheese with a firm rind and lots of medium-sized holes. It is made from cow's and sheep's milk and usually sold lightly smoked.

TEASAJT

HUNGARY

Recently developed, this loaf-shaped soft cheese has an ivory-coloured body and washed rind. It is made from cow's milk, has a sour but pleasant taste and a spicy smell. The name means 'tea cheese'.

TELEMEA

ROMANIA

The most popular cheese in Romania: a soft, white, brined type very like FETA, known as TELEMES in northern Greece. Made mainly from sheep's milk, it is sometimes spiced with cumin.

SIRENE

BULGARIA

Yet another white, brined cheese, accounting for 75% of Bulgarian cheese production. It is basically similar to the BRYNDZA cheese found throughout Eastern Europe. The version made from sheep's milk is semi-hard, rindless and rather crumbly, and kept in containers of brine making the flavour sharp and salty. But the cow's-milk version is milder.

CHANAKH (JEREVANSKY)

SOVIET UNION

A distinctive semi-hard, white, brined cheese from Armenia. Moulded into large soft-edged cubes, like giant dice, and ripened in tins, it has a sharp flavour.

SCANDINAVIA

GAMMELOST

NORWAY

An ancient cheese with a fearsome reputation, thought to date back to the Vikings. It comes in rank-smelling cylinders with dark, crusty rinds; the semi-hard cheese inside is richly veined with a blue-green mould. The name means 'old cheese', but it is actually made quite quickly, by storing the cylinders in a very damp atmosphere for a month. This encourages lush furry mould growth on the outside which is worked back into the cheese. Fat content is very low – 4–5%.

HERRGÅRDSOST

SWEDEN

A popular cheese modelled on EMMENTAL but milder. The name means 'home farm cheese' but it is now largely factory-made. Fat content is 30%, or 45% if labelled Elite. A foil-ripened version called DRABANT is eaten for breakfast.

SVECIAOST

SWEDEN

A family of 'Swedish cheeses', eaten on the scale of CHEDDAR in Great Britain or the United States. They are semi-hard, reminiscent of GOUDA and sold in many forms, both young and well-matured, with differing fat contents and sometimes with added spices.

THE MIDDLE EAST

Most native cheeses in this area are found in more than one country as they were or still are made by nomadic Bedouin.

AKKAWI

VARIOUS

Fresh, soft, white cheese, unusual for the Middle East in being made of cow's milk. Demand often exceeds supply and the shortfall is met by Danish AKAWI, made in small squares canned in brine. The taste is mild but salty.

BALADI

LEBANON

Most popular Lebanese cheese – originally made from sheep's milk, but may now include cow's. Fresh, white and crumbly; may be salted or unsalted.

BEYAZ PEYNIR

TURKEY

Named 'white cheese' this is soft and ripened in brine until it becomes very salty. Traditionally made with sheep's milk, it is very similar to Greek FETA. By far the most popular cheese in Turkey, frequently eaten for breakfast.

DUBERKI

VARIOUS

A delicacy made by Israeli and Palestinian Arabs. A LABNEH-type cheese formed into small balls, sun-dried or preserved in olive oil.

DUMYATI

EGYPT

Fresh or brine-ripened cheese made from cow or buffalo milk. Mild when fresh, strong and salty when ripened. Widely eaten in Egypt and named for a port on the Nile.

GEVINA ZFATIT

ISRAEL

Salty sheep's-milk cheese made for centuries in Upper Galilee, now part of Israel. Produced in flat discs bearing the imprint of the draining basket and usually eaten fresh.

LABNEH

LEBANON

Very simple form of cheese, little more than drained yoghurt, found under various similar names throughout the Middle East. It is made from whatever milk is locally available, and is almost liquid – the Jordanian version, LABANEH, is packed in plastic beakers.

MEIRA

IRAQ

A semi-hard to hard cheese from Iraq, made from sheep's milk, pressed and ripened for 6–12 months.

ASIA

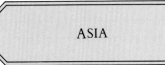

BANDAL

INDIA

Cow-or buffalo-milk cheese shaped into small balls and eaten fresh or after smoking over open fires.

DACCA

INDIA

Similar to BANDAL but pressed for 1–2 weeks before smoking to produce a firmer cheese.

SURATI PANIR

INDIA

India's best-known cheese, made from buffalo milk. The fresh white curds are ripened in whey for a few days.

KESONG PUTI

PHILLIPINES

Small, fresh, buffalo-milk cheese wrapped in banana leaves.

AUSTRALASIA

CHEEDAM

AUSTRALIA

A cross between CHEDDAR and EDAM, semi-hard and pale yellow.

KANBURRA

AUSTRALIA

Swiss-type holey cheese very similar to Norwegian JARLSBERG.

MACZOLA

AUSTRALIA

Blue cheese similar to GORGONZOLA but smaller and less rich. The cheese takes its name from the manufacturers, Macleay River Dairying Society.

EGMONT

NEW ZEALAND

A recently invented cheese, this is a cross between GOUDA and CHEDDAR.

A point, a punto: French and Italian terms indicating that a cheese is perfectly ripe.

Acid-curd cheese: one in which the curd is coagulated by the natural effect of lactic acid in the milk rather than by using rennet.

Affiné: French word describing a very well-ripened cheese.

Ammoniated: cheese that is overripe and smells or tastes strongly of ammonia.

Annatto: natural colouring obtained from the seeds of a South American tree used to dye cheese yellow or orange.

Appellation contrôlée: label carried by cheeses with protected names indicating they were made by approved methods in the designated production area. There are 27 appellation contrôlée cheeses in France. Some other countries have similar systems.

Bloom: downy, white mould growth on the surface of a cheese.

Blue (bleu): cheese with a mould culture spreading through it.

Blind: cheese with no holes or eyes in it.

Body: the inside of a cheese.

Brined cheese: one matured in a solution of salt and water.

Buttermilk: liquid left behind after cream has been churned into butter.

Caprino: general term for Italian goat's-milk cheeses.

Casein: the main protein constituent of milk.

Cendré cheese: often goat's milk, finished with charcoal or wood ash.

Cheddaring: stacking, cutting and turning curds to drain them and turn them into a dense solid mass.

Chèvre cheese: made entirely from goat's milk with a minimum fat content of 45%. *Mi-chèvre* cheese contains cow's or other milk as well.

Coagulation: the solidification of milk through the action of acids and enzymes.

Cold pack: savoury spread made by grinding up two cheeses and mixing them together, sometimes with added flvouring, without the heated process used for processed cheese.

Cooked cheese: one heated after coagulation of the curd in order to produce a firm dry body – eg EMMENTAL.

Coryne bacteria: orange-red growth produced on the surface of washed-rind cheeses.

Curd: the coagulated part of milk consisting of solid protein with some fat, a little sugar and residual whey.

Curing: ripening.

Double cream: cheese containing a minimum of 60% fat.

Dry matter: all parts of a cheese excluding the moisture: ie, fat, protein, sugar and minerals.

Eyes: small or large holes in a cheese produced by fermentation.

Evening milk: less rich milk taken from the animal at the second milking.

Farmhouse cheese: made on a farm, as opposed to in a factory, but not necessarily from unpasteurized milk. Mainly a British term.

Fat content: the proportion of fat in a cheese, expressed as a

percentage of the dry weight (fat in dry matter), not total weight. Most cheeses have a fat content of around 45–50%.

Fermier: French word for farm-produced cheese.

Flora: the mould growth that 'flowers' on the surface of cheeses like Brie.

Fresh: a cheese eaten within days, ie, unripened.

Grana: general term for hard Italian cheeses like PARMESAN.

Krauterkäse: in German any cheese containing herbs.

Lactic acid: the acid produced in milk when it turns sour.

Lait cru: French for raw milk.

Laitier: French word indicating a cheese made in a creamery from pasteurized milk.

Matière grasse: French for fat content.

Monastery cheeses: term used to describe any cheese originally invented by monks, as many were.

Morning milk: the richest milk, taken from the animal at first milking.

Non-pasteurisé: French for unpasteurized milk or cheese.

Paraffin: the waxy coating, usually red, yellow or black, on the outside of some cheeses.

Pasta filata: Italian for plastic-curd cheeses.

Paste: the body or edible part of a cheese.

Plastic curd: generic term for cheeses made by immersing the curd in hot liquid and working it until it becomes elastic and can be moulded into the shape required.

Pasteurization: heat treatment of milk to destroy micro-organisms, named after its inventor Louis Pasteur.

Pecorino: generic term for Italian sheep's-milk cheeses.

Penicillium: the family of moulds which produce white 'fur' on the surface of cheeses like CAMEMBERT (*P. candidum*), and the veining in blue cheeses (*P. glaucum*, *P. Roqueforti*).

Persillé: French term for lightly-veined cheeses (literally 'parsleyed').

Pricking: piercing of cheese to allow blue mould to spread.

Raw milk: unpasteurized milk.

Rennet: an enzyme extract obtained from the fourth stomach of a calf or other young ruminant and used to coagulate milk.

Rind: outer coating of a cheese formed by surface drying, often treated by rubbing, brining, oiling, blackening or other methods to produce the desired characteristics. Natural rinds are usually edible: synthetic rinds made by adding a layer of another substance may not be.

Ripening: synonym for maturing.

Scalding: heating curd to extract more whey.

Skimmed milk: milk which has had some of the cream removed in order to lower the fat content. It can be fully or partially skimmed.

Spun curd: see plastic curd.

Starter: a culture of acid bacteria added to milk to increase its acidity before the rennet is introduced.

String cheese: American term for plastic-curd cheese.

Surface ripened: cheese such as Brie ripened by surface moulds.

Triple cream: cheese containing at least 75% fat.

Turophile: word of Greek origin for a lover of cheese.

Unripened: synonym for fresh cheeses and whey cheeses.

Vacchino: generic term for Italian cow's-milk cheese.

Vegetarian rennet: extracts from various plants used to make vegetarian and kosher cheeses, neither of which can be made with the usual animal rennet.

Washed-rind: cheeses which are regularly treated while ripenening with liquid such as brine, water or alcohol to keep them moist and encourage the growth of coryne bacteria to give the desired yellowish-red rind.

Weeping: a Swiss-type cheese showing moisture in the holes or eyes is said to be weeping. It indicates full maturity.

Weichkäse: German generic term for surface-ripened cheese.

Whey: the liquid part of milk remaining after the curds have been separated off, it contains most of the milk sugar. Some cheeses, such as RICOTTA, are made with whey.

Whole milk: milk still containing all the original cream.

'CHEESE' IN 20 COUNTRIES

Brazil	*Queijo*	Jordan	*Jibneh*
Bulgaria	*Sirene*	Latin America (except Brazil)	*Queso*
Czechoslovakia	*Syr*	Lebanon	*Jibneh*
Egypt	*Gibneh*	Poland	*Ser*
France	*Fromage*	Portugal	*Queijo*
Germany	*Käse*	Romania	*Brinza*
Greece	*Tiri*	Scandinavia	*Ost*
Holland	*Kaas*	Soviet Union	*Syr*
Hungary	*Sajt*	Spain	*Queso*
India	*Panir*	Turkey	*Peynir*
Israel	*Gevinah*	Yugoslavia	*Sir*
Italy	*Formaggio, Cacio*		

Australia
Cheedam
Kanberra
Maczola

Belgium
Herve
Remoudou

Bulgaria
Sirene

Canada
Canadian Cheddar
Oka
Richelieu

Cyprus
Haloumi (Halloumi, Hellim)

Czechoslovakia
Liptauer (Liptauer Brindza)

Denmark
Akkawi
Blue Brie
Blue Castello
Blue Crème
Danbo
Danish Blue (Danablu)
Elbo
Esrom
Fynbo

Havarti
Maribo
Mellow Blue
Molbo
Mycella
Samsoe
Tybo

France
Banon
Beaufort
Belle Bressane
Bleu d'Auvergne
Bleu de Bresse
Bleu des Causses
Bleu de Gex
Bleu de Septmoncel
Blue Brie
Boursault
Boursin
Bondon
Boulette d'Avesnes
Brebis
Brie
Brillat-Savarin
Brin d'Amour (Corsica)
Bûche de Chèvre (Bûcheron)
Cachat
Camembert
Cantal
Caprice des Dieux
Carre de l'Est
Chabichou (Chabi)
Chaource
Chaume
Chester
Chevrette
Chevrotin des Aravis (Persillé)
Coeur de Bray
Comté
Coulommiers (Petit Brie)
Crottin de Chavignol
Cure Nantais (Fromage de
    Cure)
Demi-Sel
Epoisses
Excelsior
Explorateur
Fontainebleu
Fourme d'Ambert
Fondu aux Raisins

Fondu aux Poivres
Fondu au Kirsch
Fondu aux Noix
Fromage Blanc
Fromage Frais
Gaperon (Gapron)
Gérômé Anise
Gournay Alfiné
Livarot
Mamirolle
Maroilles
Mimolette
Morbier
Munster
Murol
Neufchâtel
Niolo (Corsica)
Pepper Brie

Petit-Suisse
PipoCrem
Poivre d'Auvergne
Pont l'Evêque
Port-Salut (Port-du-Salut)
Pyramides
Pyrénées cheese
Quatrin
Reblochon
Rigotte
Rollot
Roquefort
Roulé
Saint-Marcellin
Saint-Maure
Saint-Nectaire
Saint-Otto
Saint-Paulin
Tomme aux Raisins
Tomme Blanche

Tomme de Savoie
Valençay
Vignotte

Germany
Allgäu Emmentaler
Bianco
Blue Brie (Cambazola – brand
    name)
Butterkäse (Damenkäse)
Edelpilzkäse (Pilzkäse)
Hand Cheese (Handkäse)
Hopfenkäse (Nieheimer
    Hopfenkäse)
Limburger
Münster
Quark (Quarg)
Rahmfrischkäse
Romadur
Schmelzkäse
Smoked cheeses
Tilsiter
Weinkäse
Weisslackerkäse (Bierkäse)

Great Britain
Applewood (Charnwood)
Blue Cheshire
Botton
Blue Wensleydale
Caboc
Caerphilly
Cambridge
Capricorn
Cheddar
Cheshire
Cheviot
Colwick
Cottage Cheese
Cotswold
Cream Cheese
Crowdie
Derby
Devon Garland
Dorset Blue (Blue Vinney)
Double Gloucester
Dunlop
Huntsman
Ilchester
Lancashire
Leicester

Lymeswold
Melbury
Mollington
Nutwood
Rutland
Sage Derby
Sherwood
Shropshire Blue
Single Gloucester
Stilton
Walton
Wensleydale
White Stilton
Windsor Red

Greece
Feta
Graviera
Haloumi (Halloumi, Hellim)
Kasseri
Kefalotiri
Mizithra

Holland
Amsterdam Cheese
Commissiekaas
Edam
Friese Nagelkaas (Friesian
    Cheese)
Gouda
Kernhem
Leiden
Maasdam
Polder
White May Cheese

Hungary
Liptauer (Liptauer Brindza)
Teasajt

India
Bandal
Dacca
Surati Paneer

Ireland
Blarney

Israel
Atzmon
Bashan
Duberki
Ein-Gedi
Gad
Galil
Gilboa
Gilead
Golan
Gevina Tsefatit
Jizrael
Kol-Bee
Tal Ha'emek

Italy
Asiago
Bel Paese
Cacetti
Caciocavallo
Caciotta
Dolce Latte
Fontina (Fontal)
Gorgonzola
Grana Padano
Italico
Manteca (Burrino)
Mascarpone (Mascherpo
Mozzarella
Parmesan (Parmigiano-
    Reggiani)
Pecorino Romano
Provolone
Ragusano
Ricotta
Robiola
Stracchino Crescenza
Taleggio
Torta

Mexico
Anejo
Asadero (Oaxaca)

Middle East
Akkawi
Baladi

Beyaz Peynip
Dumyati
Labneh
Meira

New Zealand
Egmont

Norway
Gammelost
Gjetost (Getost)
Jarlsberg
Mysost (Mesost)
Nøkkelost (Kuminost)

Poland
Podhalanski

Portugal
Quiejo de Serra

Romania
Telemea

Spain
Cabrales
Cebrero
Mahon
Manchego

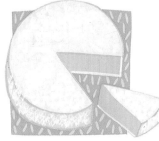

Switzerland
Alpkäse
Appenzell
Emmental
Gruyère
Raclette
Royalp
Sapsago (Schabzeiger)
Sbrinz
Tête de Moine (Bellelay)
Vacherin Fribourgeois

Sweden
Gjetost (Getost)
Herrgardsost
Mysost (Mesost)
Sveciaost

United States
American Cheddar
Baker's Cheese
Brick
Camosun
Colby
Coon Cheddar
Cooper
Cottage Cheese
Cream Cheese
Farmer Cheese
Hi-melt Cheese
Jalapeño Jack
Liederkrantz
Meunster
Monterey Jack (California
    Jack, Sonoma Jack)
New York Cheddar
Philadelphia
Pineapple
Pizza Cheese
Port Wine Cheddar
Rondelé
String Cheese (Braided
    Cheese)
Teleme
Tillamook
Vermont Cheddar
Vermont Sage
Wisconsin Cheddar

USSR
Chanakh (Jerevansky)

ADDITIONAL PICTURE CREDITS

Key: *l*=left; *r*=right; *t*=top; *b*=bottom; *c*=centre.

Courtesy of Cheese from Switzerland Ltd: pages 17 *tl bl,* 19 *bl,* 22 *tr br,* 23 *tr,* 24 *b.* Courtesy of the Danish Dairy Board: pages 21 *tr,* 23 *cb,* 47 *r,* 67. Courtesy of the Dutch Dairy Bureau: pages 9, 11, 64 *r,* 65 *l.* Courtesy of Food & Wine from France Ltd: pages 10, 23 *ct,* 48 *r.*

Jacket photographs: front, © Trevor Wood Photographer; back, courtesy of Cheeses from Switzerland Ltd.

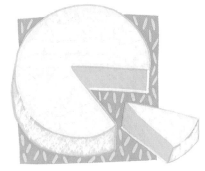